S0-BZE-456

# EQUAL RIGHTS
for Americans
with Disabilities

# EQUAL RIGHTS
for Americans
with Disabilities

## FRANK BOWE

AN IMPACT BOOK
**FRANKLIN WATTS**
NEW YORK • CHICAGO • LONDON • TORONTO • SYDNEY

Photographs copyright ©: Gamma-Liaison: frontis (Bill Greene), pp. 9 top (Szabo/Blue), 10 (Foster), 13 bottom (Shahn Kermani); Randy Matusow: p. 1; Photo Researchers, Inc.: pp. 2 (Paul Segueira), 4 bottom (Will & Deni McIntyre), 5 top (Roberta Hershenson), 5 center (Richard Hutchings), 5 bottom (Spencer Grant), 6 bottom (David M. Grossman), 8 top (Renee Lynn), 11 (Glauberman); Debi Sample: p. 3 top; Phototake, NYC/Ansell Horn: p. 3 bottom; Ben Klaffke: pp. 4 top, 7 top; The Terry Wild Studio: p. 6 top; The National Easter Seal Society: p. 7 bottom; Michael Havelin: p. 8 bottom; American Standard: p. 9 bottom; AP/Wide World Photos: pp. 12 top, 13 top, 13 center, 15 top, 16; The Lighthouse Inc.: p. 12 bottom; Gallaudet University: p. 14; Audrey C. Tiernan/Newsday/LA Times Syndicate: p. 15 bottom.

Library of Congress Cataloging-in-Publication Data

Bowe, Frank.
    Equal rights for Americans with disabilities / Frank Bowe.
        p.  cm. — (An Impact book)
    Includes bibliographical references and index.
    Summary: Describes the rights of people with disabilities in the areas of education, employment, housing, and transportation and the efforts being made to secure these rights.
    ISBN 0-531-13030-4
    1. Handicapped—Civil rights—United States—Juvenile literature. 2. Handicapped—Legal status, laws, etc.—United States—Juvenile literature.  [1. Handicapped—Civil rights. 2. Handicapped—Legal status, laws, etc.]  I. Title.  II. Series.
KF480.Z9B69   1992
346.7301'3—dc20
[347.30613]                         92-25484 CIP AC

# CONTENTS

# EQUAL RIGHTS
## for Americans
## with Disabilities

# AMERICANS WITH DISABILITIES

"**B**efore my accident, the thought of there being people out there with disabilities never entered my mind. I was the kind of person who would avoid eye contact whenever I encountered a person in a wheelchair. I was frightened of them. After the accident, I began to see how prejudiced I had been.... Now I look at people, not through them....

"Your life is changed forever. You find yourself looking within to see if you have 'the right stuff' because this kind of trauma can make you or break you....

"I found strengths inside myself I never dreamed were there."[1]*

● ● ● ● ● ● ● ● ● ● ● ● ● ● ● ● ● ● ● ● ● ● ● ● ● ● ● ● ● ● ● ● ● ● ● ● ● ● ● ●

One American in every seven has a disability. Of our nation's 250 million citizens, some 36 to 43 million have physical, mental, emotional, or sensory disabilities. Disabilities are most common among middle-aged and older Americans, least prevalent among children.[2] As the 75-million-strong baby boomer generation — those born between 1947 and 1964 — ages, the number of disabled Americans is expected to grow by another 8 million.[3]*

---

*Sources used more than once within a chapter are given the same number.

## A Growing Population

Contrary to popular belief, the number of Americans with disabilities is increasing, not decreasing. That is because many people who once died from accidents or severe illnesses now live, but with disabilities. Each year, some 500,000 Americans are in auto, motorcycle, and sporting accidents leaving them with traumatic brain injuries (TBIs); 90,000 of these are severe enough to cause permanent disabilities.[4] Illnesses producing high fevers once killed children; today, the children live, but often with limited hearing, vision, or other faculties.[5]

## Not Working

"Not working is perhaps the truest definition of what it means to be disabled," said a recent report.[6] Among working-age adults who have disabilities, just one in every three is in the labor force, that is, working or actively seeking work. Although adults aged 16–64 who have disabilities are just less than 9 percent of the nation's working-age adults, they account for 30 percent of all 16–64 year-old Americans who are not in the labor force.[3]*

Many adults with disabilities are poor. Given the low levels of employment, it is not surprising that 28 percent of adults with disabilities have below-poverty incomes. Three in ten receive federal and state assistance based on disability.

These figures illustrate how the population of Americans with disabilities is an important group in America. Disabled people are one in every ten school students, so they matter in education. Three out of every ten unemployed Americans is a person with a disability, so alleviating unemployment in our country means confronting discrimination on the basis of disability. And one-fourth of all poor adults are disabled, so eradication of poverty in America must include addressing the needs of people with disabilities.[3]

A large part of the solution is to enforce civil rights

protecting people with disabilities against unjust discrimination. That's what this book is about.

## Civil Rights

Few Americans are aware how very recent are the rights of people with disabilities. The right to an education in the public schools dates from 1977. The right to receive fair consideration for admission into colleges also began in 1977. The right to fly on an airplane was not assured until 1986. The right to fair treatment in housing was first established in 1988. The right to ride on buses equipped to accommodate people using wheelchairs came in 1990. The right to nondiscriminatory treatment in employment with most private companies in America first took effect in 1992, as did the right to enter into and enjoy the facilities of shopping malls, stores, hotels, restaurants, and movie theaters.

Prominent among the recent laws protecting disabled people is the 1990 Americans with Disabilities Act. This law forbids employment discrimination on the basis of disability by companies with more than fifteen workers. It also requires that all new buses be accessible to people with physical disabilities and that telephones be usable by deaf people. The ADA requires "places of public accommodation," such as restaurants, hotels, stores, movie theaters, and parks, to be accessible to and usable by people with disabilities. Rules explaining the ADA's many provisions appeared in summer 1991. It will take time for these rules to become effective throughout the country. When they do, however, the quality of life enjoyed by Americans with disabilities will improve tremendously.

## Social Security Programs

When people cannot live independently because they face barriers and discrimination at every turn — as people with disabilities still do — the costs to society are

**11**

high. In the case of Americans with disabilities, federal and state aid programs provide subsistence-level support for those who are not working. About three million 16- to 64-year-old adults with disabilities receive Supplemental Security Income (SSI) benefits. The federal benefit in this guaranteed-minimum-income program is some $400 per month (the states supplement this amount). The SSI program costs the federal government some $12 billion annually. In addition, SSI beneficiaries usually receive Medicaid, food stamps, and other entitlements, including housing and other subsidies, worth tens of billions more each year.

Another five million under-65 disabled adults receive Social Security Disability Insurance (SSDI) checks, many getting Medicare as well. Federal spending on SSDI exceeds $24 billion annually, with Medicare for SSDI beneficiaries adding tens of billions more each year.

A recent study suggests that two-thirds of disabled adults receiving SSI and SSDI assistance would rather be getting paychecks.[6] When their civil rights are finally implemented, many may in fact go to work. As workers, they will support themselves, pay taxes, and save the government billions each year.

### Disabilities
*Learning disabilities* such as dyslexia (difficulty reading words) and dysgraphia (problems reading maps or other illustrations) are very common. An estimated 4.5 percent of all schoolchildren have learning disabilities. Of all children receiving special education services in the public schools, half are learning disabled.[2] No one knows how many adults have learning disabilities.

In many cases, the causes of learning disabilities are unknown. Alcohol and drug use by the mother during pregnancy are suspected to be contributing factors. Occasionally, learning disabilities may be inherited.[7]

Youths with learning disabilities frequently drop out of school, frustrated with their problems in the classroom. Some studies suggest that 40 percent to 60 percent of juveniles arrested for criminal behavior are learning disabled. A three-year study in Los Angeles of suicide among under-fifteen-year-old adolescents found that half had previously been diagnosed as having learning disabilities.[8] Learning disabilities do not cause criminal behavior but rather are contributing factors.

*Speech and language impairments* are the second most common disabilities in the schools. Some 23 percent of children and youth receiving special education services have these disorders. Often, speech and language therapy help to eliminate, or at least greatly reduce, such problems as stuttering, inarticulation, and the like by early adolescence. About half of all learning disabled children also exhibit speech and language problems.[2]

*Mental retardation* is a general level of functioning in which the individual demonstrates coping skills that are not appropriate for a person that age. An IQ score below 70, which is two standard deviations below the mean, usually accompanies such behavior. On IQ tests the mean, or the arithmetical average of all scores, is 100.

About 1 percent of all live births are infants with retardation. Trisomy 21, a condition in which there is an extra twenty-first chromosome, results in Down syndrome. Most Down syndrome children and adults are moderately retarded. In about half of all persons who are retarded, however, the cause is not known. Suspected common causes include alcohol (when the mother drinks heavily during pregnancy), exposure to lead (which may be present in paint at the home or at school, and until recently was also present in many car gasolines), and malnutrition.[9]

Individuals who are retarded commonly exhibit short attention spans, difficulty with short-term memory (long-term memory, however, is relatively unaffected), and problems applying knowledge to new situations. About half are mildly retarded, with IQs in the 50/55 to 70/75 range. Relatively few are profoundly retarded, with IQs below 35.

*Emotional disturbances* affect about 1 percent of all school-age children and youth.[8] They are most common in adolescence, the same years that speech and language disorders tend to diminish.[2] Relatively few preteen children have these disabilities. Among adults, neuroses, or mild emotional disorders, are common. Less prevalent is schizophrenia, a severe emotional disability, in which people may "hear voices" or believe that the environment holds personal messages. Autism, the disability portrayed in the motion picture *Rain Man*, is rare. Most autistic children also are mentally retarded. An "autistic aloneness" is characteristic: there is an aversion of eye gaze and a lack of responsiveness to others as people.[10]

*Physical disabilities* such as cerebral palsy, paraplegia, and quadriplegia are relatively uncommon among school students. Cerebral palsy is almost always present at birth, usually as a result of oxygen deprivation before, during, or after birth. The motor control functions of the brain are affected, resulting in loss of voluntary control of many important muscles. Paraplegia, in which the voluntary control of the legs is lost, occurs when the spinal cord is injured. In quadriplegia, control of the arms and hands is also affected. Common causes of paraplegia and quadriplegia, which together affect about one-half million Americans, include accidents using automobiles or motorcycles, diving accidents, and sports accidents, usually football or basketball. Although as many as ten million Americans of all ages have physical disabilities, only one million use wheelchairs at any given time.

Multiple sclerosis is a common physical disability. About 500,000 Americans have MS. Most will never need a wheelchair. The disease is usually contracted, perhaps from a virus, during the 15 to 25 age period, but may remain dormant for as long as twenty-one years. Thus, it begins to show symptoms — fatigue, blurred vision, movement difficulty, tingling sensation or "pins and needles" in the legs — at about age 36 to 46. The single most common symptom is fatigue. Although 90 percent work prior to symptoms appearing, just 25 percent work after symptoms appear, usually because they don't have the energy. MS is probably the single most unpredictable neurological disease: its effects come and go, sometimes lasting for six months and then disappearing for three months.[11]

Much less common is muscular dystrophy (MD), made famous by Jerry Lewis's Labor Day telethons. "Jerry's kids" have an inherited disease, probably sex-linked because it occurs almost always in boys. About 20,000 boys and young men have MD.[12] The disease begins with tiny leaks in the muscle membranes. Calcium then enters the muscle cells through these leaks, activating enzymes that proceed to destroy the muscle. Muscle weakness in the lungs can lead to premature death, often by age twenty. Recent research suggests that the absence of a protein, which the scientists identifying it called dystrophin, causes muscles to deteriorate. No cure has yet been found. However, in 1991 a ten-year-old with MD received dystrophin-making genes through an injection, suggesting that a cure may come soon.[12]

*Epilepsy* is a disability in which electrical "storms," or discharges, occur in the brain. In petit mal epilepsy, momentary gaps in attention occur. In grand mal epilepsy, however, a full-scale seizure may occur in which the individual loses consciousness. As many as two million Americans have epilepsy. Most control the condition with drugs such as Dilantin, Tegretol, and Depakene. Individuals with epilepsy who have been seizure-free for five years may qualify for driver's licenses.[13]

*Sensory disabilities* include deafness and blindness. Deafness is the inability to hear and understand conver-

**15**

sational speech through the ear alone. On an audiogram, it would appear as a 90 dB (decibel) or greater loss in the better ear. Hard-of-hearing children can hear speech but usually need a hearing aid or other device. Losses of hearing are uncommon among children and youth. About 56,000 children aged 6–21 are deaf or hard-of-hearing.[2] However, severe hearing loss is so common in old age that a total of some two million Americans are deaf.

Blindness is 20/200 vision in the better eye after correction; that is, a blind person looking at a Snellen chart (the standard eye chart with rows of letters and numbers) would have to stand within twenty inches of the chart to read the letters someone with unimpaired vision could read from two hundred inches away. Low vision is 40/200 vision or worse (again after correction) or tunnel vision, which is impaired peripheral sight. About 26,000 children aged 3–21 are blind or have low vision. As with deafness, vision impairment is much more common among older adults. Two-thirds of all blind Americans are over sixty-five years of age. Virtually everyone reaching eighty years of age has a vision impairment that glasses or contact lenses cannot correct.[5]

*Traumatic brain injury* is one of the nation's fastest-growing disabilities.[14] Usually caused by accidents, often in 16- to 24-year-olds with active life-styles featuring fast driving and participant sports such as football or basketball, TBI often produces long comas.[15] Although much progress has been made recently in helping TBI individuals to regain lost functions, permanent difficulties frequently remain, most often in recall of new information.[16]

*AIDS* is emerging as another rapidly growing disability. The Americans with Disabilities Act formally recognizes people showing symptoms of AIDS as disabled persons. The disease, which first appeared in

America in the early 1980s, remains fatal. However, treatment advances now allow infected persons to live for seven or more years. The latter stages are often characterized by severe physical disabilities.[17] More devastating for many people with AIDS, however, are the fear-induced actions of employers and others: fear-based discrimination is now outlawed by the ADA. However, people who use illegal drugs are not protected by the act.

What do these disabilities mean in daily life? That's what we turn to in the next chapter.

# ABILITY AND DISABILITY

" **A** n Austin, Texas man with cerebral palsy and mental retardation had been confined to the Austin State School for many years....

"[H]e was chosen to live in a transitional independent living facility, where he was fully successful. After the one year limit for participation, he moved to his own apartment in the community, where he managed his affairs with competence, and applied for numerous jobs for which the Texas Employment Commission considered him to be qualified. After several months of rejection by prospective employers, he could no longer afford to maintain himself in the community, and was forced to return to the state institution at a far higher cost to the public than eliminating the discriminatory barriers to his productive participation in the community."[1]

In summer 1991, the respected public opinion polling firm Louis Harris & Associates conducted a telephone poll of 1,257 adults aged eighteen or over.[2] The Harris firm asked them a series of questions about their attitudes toward Americans with disabilities. The results, coming one year after enactment of the Americans with Disabilities Act, the historic civil rights bill, were revealing.

According to the study, almost half of all Americans know at least one person who is disabled — a friend, a relative, a neighbor, a coworker. That's not surprising: in a nation of 250 million people, a minority as large as 36 million is a presence in every city and county.

An overwhelming 81 percent of the Harris respondents believe that under-sixty-five adults with disabilities want to work, support themselves, and live independently — and 78 percent recognize that discrimination prevents many from doing so, as happened to the man in Austin. The general public, according to the Harris poll, strongly favors elimination of discrimination wherever it exists: 82 percent of the respondents believe employers should remove barriers to work by people with disabilities. Nine in every ten expressed strong support for the ADA's provisions.

Public support for removal of barriers facing individuals with disabilities is not new. A 1978 survey by another polling firm, Yankelovich, Skelly and White, found that 79 percent of 2,224 randomly chosen American adults favored "special efforts" on behalf of people with disabilities.[3] That support was instrumental in encouraging Congress to forge the civil rights protections now in place for Americans with disabilities. The strong public support for ADA likewise will facilitate implementation of these new rights.

Civil rights for people with disabilities are based on the idea that these are people with abilities. Given a chance, they can work, support themselves, and live independently. The Americans with Disabilities Act and other civil rights laws prohibit barriers that would prevent them from doing so. The American public believes that such fairness makes sense. That's why they support these civil rights laws.

**The Legal Definition of Disability**

An individual with a disability is a person who meets one or more of three criteria. The first is having "a physical or mental impairment that substantially limits one or more of the major life activities of such individual." The second is having "a record of such an impairment." And the third is "being regarded as having such an impairment." This three-part definition was first articulated in 1974, in the Rehabilitation Act Amendments of that year, and it was adopted again in the ADA.[4] The nation has had many years of experience with this definition.

The words "substantially limits" are understood to mean that the impairment is a severe one. People who cannot hear speech, that is, who are deaf, are "substantially limited"; on the other hand, people who have a mild hearing loss that is easily corrected with a hearing aid do not meet the "substantially limits" test. "Major life activities" include working, going to school, and getting around in the community.

The "record" test is one that applies to people who once were disabled but now have recovered. Many formerly mentally ill individuals, for example, have benefited from therapy and now are "mentally restored." It would not be fair to these people were employers and others to continue to discriminate against them just because at one time in the past they were disabled. Prior to the ADA, only the government, companies doing contract work for federal agencies, and nonprofit organizations with federal grants were required by federal law to avoid discriminating against individuals with a record of having had a disability.

The third and final test, that of "regarded as," covers people who are not disabled but falsely are thought to be people with disabilities. A good example might be someone who tests positive for the human immunodeficiency virus (HIV) but does not yet show any symptoms of AIDS. This person is not yet disabled. Forbidding this person to work or to shop would be discriminatory. Another example would be someone who wears a hearing aid, but with it hears well. Were an employer to arbitrarily reject that person's job application on the false basis that "you can't use the telephone," that, too, would be discriminatory. Again, until ADA, federal law prohibited such actions only in the case of agencies, contractors, or grant recipients.

## Disability Means Diversity

Although they share the characteristic of being individuals with a disability, disabled Americans are a remarkably diverse lot. Disability is something that usually happens to people at some point during their lives; just one in every five disabled Americans was born disabled. At any age, the likelihood that someone will become disabled is greater than the chance that they will die. Seen in this light, disability is a normal part of life.

Black Americans are much more likely than are white or Hispanic Americas to be disabled. One African-American in every seven — 14 percent — has a disability, as against just 8 percent of whites. Persons of Hispanic origin may be of any race. They have an 8 percent disability rate in the 16–64 population, or slightly higher than the white rate. The reasons for the higher rate of disability among blacks have to do with class more than with race: lower incomes translate into less medical care, poorer nutrition, less education. Lower levels of education, in turn, lead to physically demanding, often dangerous, jobs; these jobs, in turn, expose workers to more risk of accident, and thus disability, than do jobs requiring higher levels of education.[5]

Americans with disabilities tend to be less well educated, on average, than other adults. That reflects, in large part, the fact that nationwide fair admission for applicants with disabilities dates only to 1977. However, as suggested above, another phenomenon is at work: people with lower levels of education are more likely to become disabled after leaving school. Thus, when we say that levels of education among disabled Americans are lower than are those among nondisabled adults, we are including both people who are disabled in part because they were not well educated and people who are not well educated because they were disabled when they were in school. Overall, people with a disability represent 22 percent, or more than one-fifth, of all 16–64-year-old Americans with less than a high-school education.[5]

Adults with disabilities are less likely to be married but more likely to be divorced, widowed, or separated. These facts illustrate some of the stress accompanying life with a disability. Marriages are most likely to be successful when partners have secure jobs and good incomes. Until the ADA, discrimination on the basis of disability was too widespread in America for many adults with disabilities to enjoy either.

More than 2.5 million American veterans have disabilities, many from service in World War II, the Korean conflict, the Vietnam War, or the Persian Gulf War. In fact, of all men with disabilities, 39 percent are veterans.[5]

Poverty is a major problem among people with disabilities. About three in every ten have below-poverty incomes. That is triple the rate among nondisabled adults.[5]

### Attitudes Toward People with Disabilities
The 1991 Harris poll found that Americans are very conscious of how people with disabilities differ one from another. Asked if they were "comfortable" meeting someone with a disability, more than half said "Yes" about someone using a wheelchair, just under half said "Yes" about someone who is blind, and 39 percent reported being comfortable around a deaf person. However, few expressed comfort about meeting an individual who was mentally ill or retarded.[2]

The emotions most people express about individuals with disabilities are admiration and pity. The general public expresses recognition of the barriers people with disabilities confront each day. According to the Harris poll, three-quarters of the public knows that disabled people would like to be more integrated into community life than they are now, that barriers and lack of equal opportunity bring financial hardships for individuals with disabilities, and that the social life of an individual with a disability often is less fulfilling than is that of someone with no disability. Knowing these things, the general public both pities disabled people because of their problems and admires them for their perseverance in the face of these problems.[2]

The Harris poll found that most Americans believe that barriers to full participation in society were markedly lower in 1991 than they were in 1981. Fully 85 percent believe disabled people have more opportunities today than ever before.

Interestingly, the Harris poll reveals that the American public still thinks of people with disabilities as fundamentally different from other people. Said the Harris firm:

The public is unlikely to ever view people with disabilities as the same as the rest of the population, nor would this appear to be a bar to support for increasing their participation. The public wants to help disabled people precisely because they are different.... Support for special programs for disabled people rests on the public's recognition and acceptance of disabled people as different, not any less human, but with additional needs as a result of their condition.[6]

### Drugs and Disability

Disability in the 1990s has a changing face. Ever-larger numbers of children are becoming disabled as a result of maternal, and in some cases paternal, abuse of controlled substances. In years past, when most disability was caused by accidents and illnesses or by heredity, the general public could understand that the person with a disability was not "at fault" for the condition. That is, the average American understood that factors and events beyond human control were involved, and thus could readily support requests from people with disabilities for social support. That is changing now.

Some ten million Americans are chronic abusers of illegal drugs. Of them, more than half are women.[7] Some women using crack cocaine are mothers of young children. Since the start of the cocaine epidemic in 1986, some 400,000 children have been born to cocaine-addicted mothers. Some estimates indicate that the number of so-called "crack babies" may mushroom to four million by the year 2000.[8] One report suggests that more than one-third of these crack babies have brain lesions (holes) as a result of maternal crack abuse. Symptoms of crack babies include a smaller than normal head, heart defects, and enlarged kidneys. In school, these children exhibit learning problems including a short attention span, inability to identify colors, and in some cases mental retardation.[9]

Arguably, the mothers of these children are disabling them. Some experts say that crack use stifles maternal instincts.[10] Others argue that causation is irrelevant and that the issue is how to help the innocent children.[11] Some recent studies dispute whether the disabilities the children suffer are crack-related at all.[12]

Meanwhile, evidence is steadily accumulating that alcohol abuse is a powerful cause of disability. Among Native Americans, for example, chronic alcoholism is said to produce children who are unable to learn cause-and-effect relationships.[13,14] Some studies even suggest that drinking by the father prior to conception may cause retardation or other disabilities in the fetus.[15]

Disabilities caused by parental addiction to drugs or to alcohol appear to be in another category altogether from disabilities resulting from accidents or other uncontrollable factors. Will the American public's strong support for social spending on behalf of people with disabilities, including very high special education costs, survive the average American's qualms about paying for the consequences of illegal drug abuse and alcoholism?

Another issue is whether the parents' right to privacy outweighs any public interest in the health of their children. Does a woman's right to privacy outrank her unborn child's right to a healthy start in life?

## Genetics and Ethics

Today it is possible to identify more than two hundred disabling conditions during the first three months of pregnancy.[16] First-trimester fetuses with retardation,[17] some learning disabilities, multiple sclerosis,[18] muscular dystrophy,[19] and other conditions can be identified with techniques such as chorionic villus sampling (CVS). Within a few years, a simple blood test is expected to become available that also will identify disability in a fetus. Also coming soon are "genetic engineering" methods that soon are expected to allow doctors to go into the DNA (deoxyribose nucleic acid) of a fetus, remove a gene, and repair or replace it.[20,21]

These technologies are raising difficult ethical questions. At present, the only choice a woman given information suggesting that her fetus is disabled has is whether to abort.[22] Some women are choosing abortion rather than give birth to a child with a disability. Within a few years, another choice will become available, that of "fixing" the fetus to remove the gene or genes that would cause disability or to alter those genes.[23]

However women individually choose, the consequences may be major. At present, taxes collected from millions of American workers support public special-education programs for children with disabilities. Will the American public be willing to continue paying for special education if and when they perceive that the parents voluntarily "chose" to give birth to a child with a disability? Will insurance companies insist on seeing genetic maps of newlyweds before agreeing to accept life and health insurance policies? In time, we might eliminate all prebirth disabilities. The only remaining disabilities would be those caused by accidents and illnesses, and these might be susceptible to similar genetic engineering techniques that would eliminate them as well.

Some obvious questions may be asked about all of this: Which disabilities are severe enough to be prevented, either by abortion or by genetic therapy — and who is deciding that? Another, perhaps not so obvious: Will widespread public acceptance of abortion or genetic therapy as "solutions" for the problem of disability lead inexorably to devaluation of those people among us who are disabled? The ability to hold two contradictory beliefs at once — one that it is right to prevent disabilities and the other that people who are disabled are not in any way to be devalued — is something many of us would find hard to do. If the public consensus is that disability is not only preventable but should be prevented, what will that do to public support for rights and services for people who are disabled? Will they come to be viewed as "mistakes" or as "less than human"? These issues revolve around attempts to protect the rights of parents and prospective parents while at the same time preserving the rights of individuals with disabilities. In all probability, it will not be an easy juggling act for any of us.

# LIVING WITH A DISABILITY

**"O**n May 23, 1988, Lisa Carl, a wheelchair user with cerebral palsy, was refused admission to an accessible theater in Tacoma, Washington. An advocate who called the theater on Lisa's behalf was told, 'I don't want her in here and I don't have to let her in.'"[1]

**"I**n Africa, people stare at oddities. I like. that, I find. In the States, people are always averting their eyes.... 'If I can't see you,' the eyes sliding uneasily away from my body tell me, 'you can't be you.'"[2]

What is it like to be a person with a disability in America today? If you were to ask a dozen such individuals, you no doubt would receive twelve different answers. Most would say, however, that things are "much better" now than they were in the early 1970s. A Harris poll released in 1986 asked one thousand people with disabilities that question and got that answer.[3]

For most adults who have disabilities, growing up meant enduring indignities. It meant daily reminders that most people were made uncomfortable in your presence, preferring to "look through" you rather than to acknowledge you as a fellow citizen. At times, it meant being barred from community activities, as happened to Lisa Carl.

Things are, however, improving. The changes in daily life for Americans with disabilities over the past generation are, in a word, staggering. The ADA, for example, prohibits the kind of discrimination Lisa experienced when she wanted to see a movie. There are many other examples. Twenty years ago, an individual using a wheelchair could not even visit his or her senator or congressman in Washington, DC, even though the U.S. Constitution assures citizens the right to see their elected representatives. Since 1974, more than $3 million has been spent to install ramps, curb cuts, and other access features on Capitol Hill. A 1991 survey found just a few remaining barriers.[4] In thousands of towns and cities nationwide, access is now easy at local government offices, libraries, schools and colleges, and other public buildings.

Twenty years ago, most children with disabilities did not attend neighborhood schools. Today, more than 90 percent do, with the others receiving specialized instruction in separate facilities.[5] The number of youths with disabilities attending college has at least doubled just in the past ten years.[6]

And attitudes of "the man on the street" have improved markedly. The 1991 Harris poll shows that most Americans have seen such movies as *Children of a Lesser God* (about a deaf woman), *Rain Man*, about a man with autism), *My Left Foot* (about a writer with cerebral palsy), and/or *Born on the Fourth of July* (about a Vietnam veteran who uses a wheelchair). Almost six in every ten Americans reported watching at least one episode of the ABC-TV series "Life Goes On" (about a man with Down syndrome). Many told the Harris pollsters that watching these movies and TV shows changed their attitudes toward people with disabilities.[7]

## Childhood

For children with disabilities today, expectations are rising almost daily. A generation ago, teachers and parents alike expected little of students with disabilities; typically, these children were passed from grade to grade regardless of academic performance. In part, low expectations reflected parental and educator knowledge that America was so barrier-filled that few individuals with disabilities, no matter how hard they studied, stood much chance of becoming employed, self-supporting adults.[8] These lowered goals often had the unintended effect of adding another "disability," that of undereducation, to the burdens carried by children with disabilities. Fortunately, today many parents and educators recognize that most societal barriers to mobility by people with disabilities have been or are being removed. Many more devices are available today, too, to help the student with a disability to keep pace with schoolmates. Responding to these new opportunities, parents and teachers are spurring children to rise to the challenge of taking advantage of these chances to live a rewarding life.

A generation ago, too, the relatively few disabled children who attended public schools typically did so with no special help. It was rare, for example, that a school provided an interpreter for a deaf student, or special exercise equipment for a student with a physical disability. Prior to the mid-1970s, such accommodations were so rare that millions of children with disabilities had to go to special private schools to get that help.

Students in public schools also were subjected daily to mockery and taunts from other children. While such ridicule has not been eliminated, students, teachers, and parents alike are more sensitive to it today and discourage it more vigorously. It remains a problem, in part because teachers and administrators don't always take it as seriously as they do taunting on the basis of race or sex.[9] In time, disparaging comments should become less common. That is because the adults of tomorrow are today being exposed at school to disability, and becoming more accepting of it as well as more sensitive to the harmful effects of ridicule. Within a few years, people with disabilities will find that the bankers, storekeepers, police, lawyers, and teachers in their communities are individuals who learned in school about disability.

For most children with disabilities, the challenge of growing up is one they must meet without expecting someday to be cured of their disabilities. That does not mean giving in to the burdens imposed by disability. What it does mean is developing the abilities that remain, refining them so that they become a basis for an independent life in adulthood. Never before in American history has such independence been as realistic a goal as it is today. Powerful new laws such as the ADA ban unfair treatment just because someone is disabled. That means that what an employer uses to make job decisions is abilities: skills, knowledge, willingness to work.

The "job" of children with disabilities, then, is to study all the things other children learn and, in addition, to develop coping skills to minimize the impact of the disability. Special education, or instruction for students with disabilities, in the past focused more upon the latter, that is, upon helping children to "overcome" their limitations, than on the former, developing their abilities. Today, increasingly the emphasis is upon enabling them to maximize their skills. Special education laws require schools to "meet the unique needs" of children with disabilities. That may mean providing resource-room instruction for a student with a learning disability or even a "talking" computer for a student with cerebral palsy.

Not all of America is reacting so quickly to these changes. The Social Security Administration, a federal agency, has been particularly slow to adapt. Until 1990, it was harder for children with disabilities to qualify for Supplemental Security Income (SSI), the federal-state guaranteed minimum income program, than for adults. David Lewis, a six-year-old from Lancaster, Pennsylvania, was one child denied SSI benefits. David was born with a brain disability that was not on the Social Security Administration (SSA)'s list of fifty-seven "approved" disabilities. A February 1990 Supreme Court decision outlawed the SSA "listing" and required the agency to provide benefits to children like David.[10]

For a lucky few children, disability may be temporary. Justin Cano, a ten-year-old boy with Duchenne muscular dystrophy, a fatal disease, is one. He received an injection containing the protein-making gene he lacked. The genetic engineering that may save his life and that of forty other boys given injections in 1990 was made possible by the death of a seventeen-year old boy named Bruce Bryer. The Spokane, Washington, boy's genes were studied by University of Washington researchers. In 1987, they discovered that he lacked a protein researcher Louis Kunkel named dystrophin (after the disease). Once the protein was identified, extracting the protein-making gene from nondisabled people, and making copies of it, were readily accomplished. Such "engineered" genes are what Justin Cano received in a San Francisco hospital. The donor was his twin brother Jason.[11,12]

## Adolescence
As exciting as these rising expectations are, they do little to address the special problems of adolescence. The teen years are often painful for youth with disabilities. At a time when being similar if not identical to peers is important, these young people are undeniably different. Thus, "fitting in" with a group can be difficult. Transferring from regular to special schools is common in adolescence, possibly because many teens with disabilities prefer to be with other youth with disabilities during these years; at least in such groups they can find the acceptance they need.

Adolescence also means moving away from dependence upon parents and other adults. For youths with disabilities, the separation process may be even harder than for other adolescents, due to parental and educator concerns about their safety and well-being. Those worries often are well founded. In 1988, a thirteen-year-old girl in a wheelchair was raped twice by a forty-six-year-old man. A Florida district court convicted him, noting that she had screamed and tried to push him away. The conviction was overturned by an appeals court in February 1989, on the grounds that the law forbidding rape against "physically helpless" victims did not apply because the girl was not "helpless enough." The court's ruling, which the Florida Supreme Court let stand, was that she would have to have been "asleep, unconscious or physically unable to communicate her unwillingness to act" for the rape to be illegal under that law.[13] As this young woman's experience illustrates, disability often brings with it vulnerability to crime.

More often, though, the challenges are practical, although no less vexing. In September 1991, another thirteen-year-old girl, Brooke Ellison of Stony Brook, New York, returned to school for the first time since being hit by an automobile a year earlier. Riding in a motorized wheelchair and using a respirator to breathe for her, Brooke was determined to continue her education. During a year at a rehabilitation facility in New Jersey, she had studied at home, maintaining an A average in her studies. Brooke didn't know how long she could remain in school, because someone had to watch her respirator. "If the respirator stops, that's it," said her mother, who accompanied her to school because the family's medical insurance would not cover the estimated $38,000 annual cost of a private nurse at school. Nonetheless, Brooke is determined to go to college and eventually to open a rehabilitation center on Long Island.[14]

34

## Adulthood

Today's children and adolescents who have disabilities can look forward to an adulthood in which their rights will be respected. Many, too, will benefit from high technology devices now being developed. For disabled adults of today, however, the fact that the meaning of disability is changing means many are caught in the middle.

Four days after she was married, Virginia Gallego, a student at San Joaquin Delta College, in California, was in her car when a van struck it. She was in a coma for two weeks, and in the hospital for two months. Virginia was unable to remember from day to day. "The nurses had to tape my home phone number onto the dresser so I could call my new husband," she recalls. For months stretching into years, she struggled to overcome a traumatic brain injury:

My husband Al had to feed me, bathe me and take me to the bathroom. All I could do was stay home, eating and sleeping. Everything was such an effort. I couldn't sit and watch a program for more than a few minutes. Even a 30-second commercial was too much of a strain on my brain.

After three years of rehabilitation, she recovered enough of her faculties to attend college and train for a career in word processing.[15]

Ten years ago, Virginia most likely would have died from that kind of a traumatic brain injury. Ten years from now, someone having an identical injury may recover much faster, due to improved medical technology. Virginia is somewhat in the middle: she's surviving, but the state of the art in rehabilitation is not able to do nearly enough to help her.

In some cases, the transition is one of rights that are not yet fully implemented. Jay Gusler, a twenty-six-year-old laid-off construction worker, was denied employment with the Long Beach, New York, police department because of a slight hearing loss in one ear. Despite having the third-highest score on the local civil service examination, Gusler was told in August 1991 that he would not be hired. The reason given was fear by the police department that his hearing loss would interfere with his understanding speech while driving a squad car with sirens and radio noise in the background. Gusler denied his slight loss would cause any problems.[16]

Gusler was frustrated. He had the education, training, and physical strength needed to qualify for the job, yet lost it for reasons beyond his control. Officials knowing little about hearing loss, he said, acted on their fears of what a hearing impairment might mean rather than on the facts. Gusler filed a complaint with the state human rights commission, alleging discrimination. A year later, he would have been able to use the ADA, which became effective in July 1992, and might have won. More important, as attitudes toward disability improve, he might never have been mistreated at all.

The kinds of barriers Gusler faced in Long Beach were for years daily obstacles for millions of adults with disabilities. Sometimes the accumulated frustrations led to bitterness. Robert Chesney, fifty-nine, of Los Angeles, who became deaf at age ten from spinal meningitis, earned a BA degree from Gallaudet College (now University). Because few careers were open to deaf people in the 1950s, he became a printer at the Long Beach (California) *Press-Telegram*. In those days, employers routinely used the rationale "the noise won't bother them" to justify segregating deaf workers in jobs operating noisy equipment. Despite his college degree and years of experience, Chesney didn't get promoted. He was passed over time and time again by hearing subordinates and coworkers. Again, the employer's rationale was that higher-paying jobs required the ability to hear.

There were no laws at the time, the 1960s and 1970s, prohibiting such discrimination.

Eventually, Chesney became bitter. Injured on the job one day in the early 1980s, he left and enrolled in Social Security Disability Insurance (SSDI), the federal program for disabled ex-workers. In 1982, he took the additional step of suing the *Press-Telegram* for discrimination. Five years later, he settled the case out of court for a onetime payment of $150,000 and an annual supplement of $20,000.

That was just the start. In July 1991, federal agents searched his apartment in a Los Angeles federally subsidized housing project for disabled and elderly people. They found sixteen boxes and three steamer trunks filled with fake birth certificates, bank statements, and Social Security cards. Chesney allegedly had ripped off the federal government by enrolling in SSDI under twenty-nine different names. In September 1991, he pleaded not guilty to eighteen felony counts of filing false claims.[17]

Deaf people today seldom are shuttled to dead-end jobs where "your hearing doesn't matter." Rather, they're being given the chance to develop their skills in meaningful occupations. Each year, fewer and fewer deaf adults are as frustrated as was Robert Chesney. But for some, the changes come too late: they have settled into a life-style of dependency, from which they do not feel they can escape. "Rocky," a forty-five-year-old former fence installer who contracted multiple sclerosis in 1979, lives in the garage of his own home in Brentwood, New York. Since 1985, he's been using a motorized wheelchair. Rocky survives on SSDI checks and rental of the rest of his house. He has no telephone. If he needs something, he bangs on the wall. Most days, he watches television and listens to a large supply of gospel music tapes. Living "on the other side," to use Rocky's words, is his older brother Joey. In 1991, Joey was arrested for selling crack cocaine and running a prostitution ring from the house.[18]

Others keep going. Allison Thompson, a twenty-five-year-old travel agent, was rushing to catch a train in New York City's Penn Station when she felt her leg go numb. She missed her train. For the next three weeks, the numbness came and went. A few months later, her vision blurred. She soon became blind. No longer able to function as a travel agent, she left her job. The diagnosis of multiple sclerosis followed. But Thompson didn't let it stop her. Returning to the family demolition business, she found she could work when the "pins and needles" did not prevent her from using a pen or typing. In 1990, the six-foot Levittown resident won the Miss Long Island beauty pageant. She's using her title to increase public awareness of MS.[19]

Allison represents the promise of the near future. Taking advantage of new rights, she's continuing to work. Because she works, she's able to live independently. And she offers a model to today's children with disabilities. These children see adults functioning well despite disability, working at rewarding jobs, owning their own homes and cars. Twenty years ago, such models were hard to find. Today, they're in every American community. The message they send to children with disabilities is: "If I can do it, you can do it."

# EQUAL RIGHTS IN EDUCATION

"**I**n Rochester, New Hampshire, Timothy, a multipl[y] disabled young boy with learning problems so severe that school officials thought he was unable to benefit even from intensive special education, nonetheless won the right to a free public education."[1]

"**C**arolee Reiling, a student at Stanford University, first recognized that she had a learning disability when she listened to another student's story. By meticulously noting each problem she had, and each coping strategy that helped her, she managed to do well at that highly selective school."[2]

"**A**lison Sutton wasn't so lucky. 'It wasn't until after college that I learned about assistive listening systems, my legal rights to a note-taker, and about the Disabled Student Services Office on campus,' said the hard-of-hearing graduate."[3]

A federal law guarantees a free, appropriate public education in the least restrictive environment to all children with disabilities, from birth to age twenty-one. The Individuals with Disabilities Education Act, popularly called IDEA, is a "zero reject" law: no child, no matter how disabled, even as severely as is Timothy, may be denied an education. To the maximum extent appropriate, the child is to be taught in neighborhood schools. He or she must receive needed accommodations so that the education received is at least minimally acceptable. And parents may use due process, including lawsuits, to protect his or her rights.[4]

A 1973 statute, implemented in 1977, provides protection for youth and adults with disabilities in postsecondary education. Section 504 of the Rehabilitation Act of 1973 does not (unlike IDEA) guarantee instruction for students with disabilities. Rather, it forbids discrimination by two-year and four-year colleges and universities. Only youths and adults with disabilities who meet eligibility criteria for admission in these postsecondary programs are protected. They are entitled to such reasonable accommodations as sign-language interpreters in the classroom, texts and other instructional materials in Braille or large print, and counseling as needed.[5]

### Public Education

According to the U.S. Department of Education, 4,687,620 children with disabilities were served in the public schools during the 1989–1990 school year. About one public-school student in every ten is a child with a disability.[6]

Federal and state laws provide that local school districts be reimbursed for the "excess costs" they incur in educating children with disabilities. Excess costs are expenses in addition to those spent on the average, nondisabled child in that school district. In the 1986–1987 school year, federal, state, and local governments paid some $17 billion to educate children with disabilities, or about $4,000 per child. State governments paid some 56 percent of these excess costs, with local governments picking up 36 percent and the federal government 8 percent. The federal share was about $350 per child.[7] These "excess costs" are expenses over and above what the school districts spend on nondisabled students. Thus, teaching a student with a disability averages some $10,000 per year.

## Preschool Services

Federal law assures that public services are available, at no cost to the parents, from birth or when the disability is first diagnosed. IDEA has two sections, known as Part H and Part B, explaining how states are to accomplish this purpose.

Part H of IDEA serves infants and toddlers who have disabilities, are delayed in their development, or are at risk for becoming disabled. Family support services, counseling, and early intervention therapy are offered to all such children under three years of age. An Individualized Family Services Plan (IFSP) is developed for each child, outlining who will provide what services. All fifty states served 0–2 year-olds with disabilities during the 1991–1992 school year.

Part B of IDEA includes a Preschool Grants Program which provides services for children aged 3–5. Of the fifty states, forty-seven served 3- to 5-year-olds during 1991–1992. The other three states are expected to begin services in 1992–1993, or shortly thereafter.

Although many of these children receive educational services for only half the school day, costs often are higher than are those for elementary and secondary education. In New York's Long Island, for example, local schools spend an average of $16,000 per child, plus $7,000 for transportation. The island's two counties together spend $100 million annually teaching 3- to 5-year-old preschoolers with disabilities. Costs are so high because state regulations restrict each class to a maximum of eight students, because most children receive speech and physical therapy in addition to classroom instruction, because many also need services from psychologists and social workers, and because special equipment often is needed.[8]

### Elementary and Secondary Education

IDEA defines the term "special education" as "specially designed instruction...to meet the unique needs of a child with a disability." This may include regular classes, but it may also include separate classes or resource rooms. In addition, children with disabilities are entitled to "related services" including special transportation, counseling, and therapy related to their disabilities. These special education and related services are outlined in an annual Individualized Education Program (IEP) that is prepared for each child. All fifty states served 6- to 18-year-olds during the 1991–1992 school year, and many served 19–21-year-olds as well.

Most students with disabilities are served in regular school buildings. A plurality receives resource room services, some three in every ten are educated in regular classrooms, and others are taught in separate classes. Relatively few are served in separate day or residential schools. Four disability categories account for 94 percent of all children and youths served by IDEA in 1989–1990. Almost half have learning disabilities. The number of students identified as having learning disabilities has soared 160 percent in the past decade. Speech/language disorders are second most common. Mental retardation is third; the number of students classified as retarded has fallen 40 percent in the past ten years, as the definition was tightened and as many children previously identified as retarded now are classified as learning disabled. Emotional disability is the fourth most-common classification. The remaining eight categories — such as deaf/hard-of-hearing, blind/visually impaired, deaf-blind, and health-impaired together account for only 6 percent of the 4,687,200 children served.[9]

## Postsecondary Education

Carolee Reiling, who was quoted at the beginning of the chapter, is one of 1.3 million college students with disabilities. According to the American Council on Education, one in every nine undergraduates has a disability.[10]

Section 504 obligates virtually all of the nation's 3,000 colleges and universities to provide nondiscriminatory admission and instruction to people with disabilities. According to a 1987 report by the College Board, "overall, admissions decisions for handicapped applicants followed quite closely what one would expect from their high school grades and SAT scores." The number of postsecondary programs providing special services to students with disabilities increased fivefold between 1977, when the section 504 regulation was published, and 1987. Today, some 2,300 colleges and universities have services for students with disabilities.[11]

## Historical Background

The laws assuring an education for people with disabilities have been in effect fewer than fifteen years. For most of America's history, and in other countries as well, children with disabilities seldom received an education.

We trace the beginning of special education to the private tutors of rich and powerful landowners in Europe. In France, the Abbé de l'Epee founded a private school in Paris for deaf children of wealthy Europeans. That was in the late 1700s. Because disabilities were fairly uncommon, schools such as his were residential (boarding) facilities. In the United States, the first such schools appeared in 1812 (in Baltimore, for blind children) and in 1817 (in Hartford, for deaf children). In 1854, at the request of reformer Dorothea Dix, Congress passed a law providing public lands for construction of schools for mentally ill, deaf, and blind children. By the end of the Civil War, a majority of states had at least one such state-sponsored special school or hospital.

By the midtwentieth century, however, many had become the huge, insensitive, very harmful institutions that Geraldo Rivera exposed at Willowbrook in the early 1970s, an exposé that to this day drives a national effort to abolish institutions.[12] It was not until after the civil rights movement of the late 1950s and mid-1960s that the idea arose that persons with disabilities are minority group members, that society has some obligations beyond physical restoration of "normality." Parents went to court in the early 1970s, demanding that their children with disabilities have access to an education in the local public schools. That led, in 1975, to what is now IDEA. For the first time in the nation's then-199-year history, children with disabilities had a right to attend public schools, to a "free, appropriate, public education."

The efforts trace to lawsuits by parents in the District of Columbia and Pennsylvania Association for Retarded Children leading to decisions based on the equal-protection clause of the U.S. Constitution. The Fourteenth Amendment, ratified in 1868, states: "No State shall make or enforce any law which shall abridge the privileges or immunities of citizens of the United States; nor shall any State deprive any person of life, liberty, or property, without due process of law; nor deny to any person within its jurisdiction the equal protection of the laws." It was not until 104 years later, however, that anyone applied that language to education of people with disabilities.

In 1972, *Mills* v. *Board of Education of the District of Columbia* brought seven children and their parents to Judge Joseph Waddy's courtroom. Three of the children lived in public residential institutions, where they received no education; the other four lived at home with their parents but were excluded from local schools. Most had behavioral disorders, were emotionally disturbed, or were retarded. They sued on their own behalf and for all disabled children in the District, saying that the District

44

had admitted in 1971 that 12,340 children with disabilities were not being served in the public schools. Judge Waddy ruled in favor of the plaintiffs, basing his decision on the Fourteenth Amendment and on the 1788 due process Fifth Amendment. He ordered a zero-reject policy such that all children would be served, either in the public schools or in an alternative setting, at local school district expense: "That the District of Columbia shall provide to each child of school age a free and suitable publicly supported education regardless of the degree of the child's mental, physical or emotional disability or impairment. Insufficient resources may not be a basis for exclusion." Judge Waddy required each child's education to be "suited to his or her needs." He forbade the school district from suspending any disabled child for disciplinary reasons "for more than two days without a hearing and without providing for his education during the period of suspension." These edicts led, in time, to the key provisions of the federal IDEA law.[13]

Also in 1972, *Pennsylvania Association for Retarded Children v. Commonwealth of Pennsylvania* saw parents of thirteen retarded children in Judge James Broderick's court in Philadelphia. The state had a compulsory education law for all children aged eight to seventeen, but had used four other state statutes to deny an education to many retarded children and youths. One such law relieved the state board of education from responsibility for any child a public school psychologist certified to be uneducable and untrainable. A second allowed an indefinite postponement of admission to public school of any child who had not attained a mental age of five years. Judge Broderick also ruled on the basis of the Fifth and Fourteenth amendments. He called for a preplacement hearing at which the parents had the right to attend, to bring with them a lawyer or other advocate, to examine all records, to introduce any evidence of their own, and to have responsible school officials present. This led to

IDEA's procedural safeguards. A Commonwealth Plan to Identify, Locate and Evaluate Retarded Children (COMPILE) was to find all such children in the state. This led to IDEA's "child find" provision. The case established the "least restrictive environment" principle, arguing that people should be free to live as they please unless they are harming others; that is, when government has a legitimate goal to accomplish, it should do so by means that curtail individual freedom to the least possible extent.[14]

The *Mills* and *PARC* decisions were mandatory, but only in the courts' jurisdictions, that is, the District of Columbia and the state of Pennsylvania. In 1975, Congress enacted the Education for All Handicapped Children Act. This act, now known as IDEA, for the first time made public education for children and youths available in every state in the nation.

Two years later, in 1977, regulations implementing section 504 of the Rehabilitation Act of 1973 appeared, establishing for the first time a right to nondiscriminatory admission and treatment in postsecondary education.

### Controversies in Education
Despite the fact that IDEA requires only an "appropriate" education, costs are very high, in some cases reaching $40,000 per child per year, or even more. State and local education agencies are bitter that the federal government, which requires them to spend such sums, contributes only an average of $350 per child per year to the cost. Educators defend the high costs by pointing to the need for "related services," including special transportation, speech and language therapy, and other noninstructional services, as well as the small size of special education classes. Critics respond, however, that transportation and other related services are not education and should not be charged to school budgets. Some also complain that at a time when tight local budgets force

curtailment of athletic activities and other services for nondisabled students, special education as well should bear its share of the burden of controlling expenses.

Complaints about costs are ironic in view of another controversy in special education. As dramatic as IDEA has been in assuring that no American child with a disability may be denied an education, the law says nothing about the quality of instruction the children must receive. Nor has any state "excellence in education" improvement program addressed the need to provide children with disabilities with a "quality" education. Concerns about quality are highlighted by evidence reported in 1990 by the U.S. Department of Education that just over half of students with disabilities tested at or above grade level in academic subjects.[15] As many as four out of every ten students with disabilities who are served in the public schools drop out without receiving a degree.[16] These dismal results hardly comport with the very high per-pupil costs. U.S. Census Bureau data on education attainment by adults with disabilities show that undereducation is a massive problem among adults as well.

As Table 1 illustrates, adults aged 25–64 are more likely to have a less-than-high-school education and much less likely to have a college degree. The data were gathered in 1989.[17]

Some controversies in education are more technical. The single most common disability in the schools today, accounting for about half of all disabled students, is learning disability. This category includes children with dyslexia, dysgraphia, and other well-defined problems dealing with information. But there is no valid and reliable test for learning disability. The law speaks of two steps in classifying children with this disability. The first is the so-called exclusion rule, under which the school first rules out any other disability (by, for example, testing hearing to rule out hearing impairment). The second

**TABLE 1**

**Education Attainment: Disabled and Nondisabled Adults Aged 25–64**

| Years Completed | Disabled | Nondisabled |
| --- | --- | --- |
| All | 100.0% | 100.0% |
| Fewer Than 8 | 14.1 | 3.7 |
| 8 | 7.8 | 2.6 |
| 9–11 | 19.5 | 9.9 |
| 12 | 35.8 | 40.7 |
| 13–15 | 14.2 | 19.0 |
| 14+ | 8.7 | 24.1 |

is the "discrepancy rule," under which only students who test significantly lower in one particular area than in others are to be classified as learning disabled. A dyslexic child, for example, would test much better if asked questions orally and permitted to respond by speaking than he or she would in a pen-and-paper test.

The reality, however, is not as neat as this two-part definition would suggest. Over the past fifteen years, the number of children classified as learning disabled has almost tripled. At the same time, the number identified as retarded has dropped by nearly half. Are some children previously labeled retarded now being reclassified as learning disabled? The evidence seems to indicate that this is happening in some states.[18] At the same time, critics charge, many children who should be called "slow learners," that is, who have IQs in the 70–90 range, are being classified as learning disabled so that the state, and the local school, may receive federal funds to educate these children. The evidence on that point is inconclusive, but anecdotal evidence suggests that it may be occurring in some states.[19]

"Mainstreaming," which reached a peak in the late

1970s, remains controversial, especially in education for deaf students. The law expresses a strong preference for education in "the least restrictive environment." This reflects continuing abhorrence of impersonal special institutions. Local public schools, it is believed, at least are monitored more closely by the community. Abuses such as those reported at New York's Willowbrook and Pennsylvania's Pennhurst are unlikely to occur in neighborhood schools that parents and other community members visit daily.[20] But that is not how many deaf people see it. The deaf community argues that placing deaf children, who rely mostly on American Sign Language (ASL), into classrooms with hearing children actually segregates them. There may be physical proximity, but since the deaf and hearing classmates cannot talk meaningfully to each other, the effect is social isolation for the deaf child. These advocates recommend, instead, that deaf children be placed in special schools with other deaf children. Teachers, staff, and students at such schools all use ASL. Such an environment may not offer much physical proximity with hearing children, but it does provide truly meaningful communication and interaction. Special "deaf-only" schools, the advocates say, are in fact the "least restrictive environment" because there the deaf children are not restricted in communicating.[21]

# EQUAL RIGHTS IN TRANSPORTATION AND MOBILITY

"'**W**e're concerned, first, that the vast majority of the [United Bus Owners of America's] 1,000 [member bus companies] will be forced to fold in the wake of the bill's mandate that all new buses must be made 'fully accessible' to handicapped riders.'"[1]

"**S**ome disabled-rights groups contend that requiring such [24-hour] notice still denies the disabled equal access. Such groups believe cost is no object when it comes to redesigning society to fit their notions of equality. In the 1970s, they used similar arguments to call for making the aging New York subway system accessible to the disabled. Mayor Ed Koch pointed out that the costs were so enormous that it would be cheaper to provide every disabled passenger with his own car and driver.'"[2]

"'**W**hen I first saw a draft of the ADA in 1988, I thought: Are they nutty? Do they really think they can do this?… The entire time [ADA was in debate] I kept thinking, I can't believe it's really going to happen.'"[3]

"**S**ince 1968 the Architectural Barriers Act has required that bus terminals built with federal funds be accessible. But here in 1990 we're

51

still discussing whether the buses that pull into those terminals should be accessible."[4]

●●●●●●●●●●●●●●●●●●●●●●●●●●●●●●●●●●●●●●●●●●●●●

Do Americans with disabilities have a right to "get from here to there"? Until 1990, the answer often was no. In fact, ground transportation barriers were among the last to begin to fall, of all barriers preventing Americans with disabilities from living a rewarding life.

Transportation is hugely important to quality of life in the 1990s. In a typical day, the first thing an average American does upon leaving the house in the morning is to get into a personal automobile. He or she then may drive to a dry cleaning establishment to drop off laundry, to a convenience store for coffee and doughnuts, and then to work. At lunchtime, he or she may take the car to a shopping mall to buy household necessities. On the way home from work, people typically pick up groceries, stop at the bank to deposit or withdraw money, or get children from school. After dinner, they may get in the car once again to go to a movie or to see friends. Many car owners average 15,000 miles each year, or 41 miles each day, in their automobiles.

By contrast, transportation barriers of a magnitude unimaginable by most Americans confront millions of people with physical disabilities. Suppose the adult in our example were someone with quadriplegia, a physical disability that limits use of both arms and hands. For this adult, the only personal vehicle that can take a motorized wheelchair is a $40,000 minivan. If the adult lacks the financial resources to purchase such a vehicle, he or she has to rely on public transportation. Until very recently, most public transit buses were not lift-equipped. Of the country's 450 public transit systems, less than one-fifth have lift-equipped buses in service.[5,6] Making matters even worse was the fact that bus drivers often claimed that the lifts were broken, as an excuse not to stop to pick up a disabled passenger. People who are blind, and many with epilepsy, are unable to drive themselves, so also must use public transportation. For them, buses have been, and still are, more usable than for people with physical limitations.

For physically disabled Americans, public transportation still offers very limited service. In New York City, for example, the nation's largest subway remains largely inaccessible to people using wheelchairs. Says James Weisman, of the Eastern Paralyzed Veteran's Association:

> In New York City, you pay one fare no matter how far you go on the system. We have people who call our office and ask, "Do you pay by the distance you go?" And they've lived in New York their whole life; they've just never used public transportation.[3]

Tens of millions of Americans with physical disabilities are limited, instead, to so-called dial-a-ride services providing perhaps two round trips each month. Those trips must be scheduled as much as two full days in advance; no changes are permitted in destination or schedule. Somehow, people are expected to try to cram into those two monthly trips all their doctor, dentist, food, clothing, banking, and other needs. Work is out of the question: twenty round-trips, not two, are needed each month to work.[7]

The American people know that accessible transportation is important for people with disabilities. In summer 1991, for example, the Louis Harris & Associates polling firm asked 1,257 American adults chosen at random if they support the idea that "new public transportation vehicles must be accessible to disabled people." Fully 93 percent said yes. The Harris firm probed by advising respondents that "it will also in some cases be expensive." Still, 89 percent said "Yes, the cost will be worth it."[8]

One might expect that such overwhelming public support would translate into services people with disabilities can use. It will, fairly soon. But it could have, a generation ago. In what can only be described as a comedy of errors, government fumbled about for twenty years before finally stating, in the 1990 Americans with Disabilities Act, that transportation must be accessible.

As long ago as 1970, the U.S. Congress declared it to be national policy that people with disabilities have the same right to public transportation as do others. What followed was twenty years of zigzags that would be laughable were they not so tragic.

In 1973, the U.S. Congress passed the Rehabilitation Act (PL 93–112), 29 U.S.C. 701. The last sentence of that act, section 504, stated that henceforth it would be illegal for anyone to use federal grant monies in such a way as to exclude or limit participation by persons with disabilities. Billions in federal funds are given each year to states, counties, and cities to help pay for public transportation. No one disputed that section 504 applied to those funds. Nonetheless, it took the U.S. Department of Transportation four years to explain what section 504 meant for public transportation. What was required, the department said, were "special efforts." The meaning of the term, it soon became clear, was that local transit agencies were to "think about" the needs of people with disabilities and to make those changes the agency thought it could afford. The "special efforts" standard was so low as to be, for all practical purposes, meaningless.

In 1979, the department replaced the 1977 rule with a new one, requiring that transit agencies purchase wide-door, low-floor, ramp-equipped "Transbus" vehicles that even people using motorized wheelchairs could easily get on and off. In 1981, an appeals court overturned this new regulation, saying that the department had done more than section 504 allowed.[9]

Returning to the drawing board, the department

issued a new rule in 1983 calling, again, for "special efforts" on behalf of people with disabilities. The new rule included a "cost cap" — transit operators were not required to spend more than 3 percent of their operating budgets on services for persons with disabilities. This latter provision was attacked in court by Weisman's Eastern Paralyzed Veterans Association. The court, on January 4, 1989, struck down the 3 percent rule. The department was ordered to issue a new rule no later than September 21, 1990.

As the department was writing that — a full generation after Congress had first told it to make public transportation accessible — the Americans with Disabilities Act was passed. So the department published, on October 4, 1990, yet another rule, this one requiring local transit authorities to purchase accessible, lift-equipped buses. The 1990 regulation implemented both the ADA procurement requirements and section 504.[10]

Meanwhile, as this twenty-year comedy of errors was playing out in Washington, tens of millions of Americans with disabilities were left with no access to public transportation. The effects were devastating. It will take years, and billions of dollars in spending, for them to be overcome.

### Air Travel

The first form of transportation to become accessible, ironically, was the last to evolve — air transportation. Section 504 of the Rehabilitation Act of 1973 requires airports, which usually receive federal funds, to be accessible to and usable by people with disabilities. The Air Carriers Access Act of 1986 requires commercial airlines using these airports to provide nondiscriminatory services for passengers with disabilities.[11] Although implementation of the act was at first contentious, with some organizations representing blind people demonstrating against such airline practices as stowing their canes, the law is now well integrated into standard airline operating procedures.

## Commuter Bus Travel
The bus follies of 1970–1990 were finally ended in August 1990. The Americans with Disabilities Act requires all new mass-transit buses purchased after August 25, 1990, to be lift-equipped. Mass-transit buses are those commuters use for intracity (within-the-city) surface transportation. These buses also are to have priority seating signs, interior handrails, and securement locations to tie down wheelchairs. Rural bus companies, which often buy used buses rather than new ones, are to acquire lift-equipped buses unless they can show they failed despite "a good faith effort" to do so. The ADA forbids urban transit systems to purchase any inaccessible new buses. It also requires that these buses be "usable," which means that the lifts must be operational and the driver must activate them. This is important because surveys show that some 80 percent of all Americans who use public transportation to and from work ride a mass-transit bus.[12]

## Intercity Bus Travel
Intercity "over-the-road" buses used by companies belonging to the United Bus Owners of America and the American Bus Association are given, in the ADA, a six- to seven-year delay in complying. Transit expert Dennis Cannon explains why UBOA, led by Greyhound/ Trailways, lobbied for the delay:

An over-the-road coach is a bus with its floor about 50" above ground, with baggage stored underneath. Some wheelchair lifts take up baggage space. Greyhound uses its buses for package express and that makes up a fairly substantial portion of its revenue.[13]

There are other differences. According to Susan Perry, senior vice president for government relations, American Bus Association, the over-the-road bus industry is private. "The private side has never been looked at. We don't get any federal subsidies, so cost becomes a much more important factor than it is on the public side." One sensitive issue for Perry is whether the restrooms in the rear of over-the-road buses must be altered for wheelchair users. "For the restrooms to be accessible, they would need to be twice as big as they are now, and that would take away revenue-producing seats." On the plus side, Perry notes: "The driver assists everybody onto the bus, collects the tickets, shows you where the bus is, frequently puts the baggage on, and always helps the passengers on."[14] On mass-transit buses, by contrast, the driver remains seated behind the wheel while passengers embark and disembark.

EPVA's Weisman is still upset about the "Greyhound amendment":

The Greyhound thing is an outrage — Greyhound getting this exemption for six or seven years for the over-the-road style coaches. It was completely unnecessary. The Congressional committees knew it was unnecessary because Denver was testifying before the committees at the same time Greyhound was, saying that they've done this already on over-the-road coaches, and they've done it for $8,500 a bus — not the $35,000 that Greyhound was saying — that they lost no baggage space and not one seat, and that Greyhound had visited their facility and toured these buses. Greyhound just used the "big lie" policy and intimidated Congress.[15]

### Rapid Rail Travel
The Americans with Disabilities Act requires that all new rail cars and all new stations be accessible to and

usable by people with disabilities. By July 26, 1995, each train must have at least one accessible car. "Key stations," such as switching stations where people transfer from one train to another, must become accessible within three years, although extensions may be granted. Amtrak, the federally assisted train system, is given twenty years for all its stations to become accessible.

## Technical Issues and Controversies

The liveliest issue in the transportation industry is that of "securement devices." The Americans with Disabilities Act requires that ways be found to lock "common wheelchairs" during transit, so that users are not injured. However, there is no "common" wheelchair design. According to Cannon: "The securement issue is a tricky one." The three-wheeled Amigo-style chair is particularly hard to tie down. The U.S. Department of Transportation's Robert Ashby says DOT received more comment from the public on securement issues than on any other question in its ADA rulemaking process. "There was a great deal of concern," he says, that three-wheelers "wouldn't fit their securement devices, couldn't be secured properly, weren't safe, and exposed passengers to injury and transit providers to liability."[16]

Another question is how to provide embarkation for wheelchair users. The American Bus Association's Perry says that Greyhound is testing an innovative boarding chair. "It is similar to an airplane boarding chair, only better. It is much sturdier, and seems to be much easier to move." She says Greyhound also is developing a ramp: "The ramp comes out of the bus and it turns and goes along the side of the bus so that it is long enough and gradual enough for a boarding chair to be pushed, but it doesn't stick way out... It is portable. It comes apart and folds up and goes in the baggage bay and travels with the bus."[14]

In the end, people with disabilities, government,

and the transportation industry will have to work together to implement the ADA. Such cooperation would be all but unprecedented. Advocates lobbying Congress to enact the ADA say the industry was their number one opponent. They remain suspicious, as well, of the U.S. Department of Transportation. EPVA's Weisman is typical in his view of the federal regulatory agency: "DOT itself has never really been responsive to accessibility complaints. I am unaware of DOT ever coming down on a transit property for not providing transportation to the disabled. I've been doing this work since 1977. and I know of no instances of DOT being an advocate."[15]

According to Jack Gilstrap, executive vice president, American Public Transit Association (APTA), which for twenty years has vigorously opposed civil rights in mass transit, enactment of the ADA ended the fight: "The civil rights for people with disabilities which are outlined in the ADA will only become reality after a tremendous amount of hard work, planning, cooperation, and commitment of resources. I firmly believe that all APTA members will strive to carry out both the spirit and letter of the law."[17]

# EQUAL RIGHTS IN HOUSING

**6**

"**I**n the first government lawsuit charging discrimination against the handicapped in housing, the Justice Department yesterday [June 20, 1989] sued an Illinois city for refusing to grant a building permit for a group home for mentally retarded adults.... [A Justice spokesman said that] just as 'community opposition to black people in a neighborhood doesn't justify preventing blacks from living in a neighborhood, the same fears of handicapped people in the neighborhood aren't justifiable under the law now for keeping handicapped people out.'"[1]

"**T**he residents of 272 Pearl St. in North Lawrence [New York] do many of the same things their neighbors do after a hard day at work: Maria sits on her bed and listens to a Meat Loaf album.... One thing, however, sets the residents of 272 Pearl St. apart from their neighbors: they are mildly retarded.... An arsonist's work almost ended the experiment for Maria, Billy, John and Tom before the experiment began.... Investigators later discovered a bottle in the living room that had contained kerosene [a Molotov cocktail]. No arrests have been made in the case."[2]

No aspect of life is more frustrating for many people with disabilities than is housing. John Kemp, executive director of United Cerebral Palsy Associations, Inc. (UCPA), who worked for many years in Chicago, reports: "In Cook County, Illinois [the Chicago area], 10,000 young people with disabilities live in nursing homes because there are no accessible homes or apartments to be found."[3] The fact that young adults with disabilities have to move into nursing homes by the thousands speaks volumes about the inaccessibility of homes and apartments in the Chicago area. Unfortunately, the problem is nationwide in scope. Some experts estimate that only 1 percent of the country's housing stock is accessible to people with physical disabilities.[4]

That statistic points to a massive problem. People with disabilities can train for years for a job but be forced to decline one after it is offered because they are unable to find a place to live within commuting distance. Others are forced to live with their parents well into adulthood. Making matters worse is the lack of affordable housing. Widespread discrimination has depressed incomes of disabled adults for years, making it difficult for many to afford those few accessible apartments or condominiums they can find.

Private one- or two-family homes are not, and never have been, required to be accessible. Apartment buildings and condominiums were free from federal accessibility design standards until as recently as March 13, 1991. In time, a 1988 law will raise that proportion markedly. The June 1989 Illinois case illustrates that the law will be enforced. Still, the fact that the first-ever housing discrimination case benefiting people with disabilities was filed in 1989 shows how new these rights are — and how far we as a nation have yet to go.

### Fair Housing Amendments Act

The Fair Housing Amendments Act of 1988 is a landmark law. The FHAA applies to new apartments, condominiums, cooperatives, and other multifamily complexes occupied after March 13, 1991. These units are to be accessible to and usable by persons with disabilities. In time, as older buildings are replaced by new ones, the supply of accessible housing in America will greatly increase. Neither the FHAA nor state statutes require that new private single-family homes be accessible. The FHAA, however, does cover private housing with four or more units. In doing so, the 1988 act became the first federal law for people with disabilities to impose civil rights requirements on private organizations and individuals who receive no government grant funds.[5]

The act requires that new multifamily buildings and complexes be "adaptable." Adaptable housing is readily converted to make it more accessible for people with severe disabilities. For example, thermostats, light switches, and even kitchen cabinets may be lowered quickly, inexpensively, and easily. Grab bars may be readily installed in bathtubs because an adaptable home has the reinforcements in the wall to accept the bars. As another example, first- and second-floor closets are lined up so that an elevator could be installed easily if needed.

Doors, until now typically twenty-four to twenty-eight inches wide, are to be thirty-two inches wide, so as to accommodate a wheelchair user.

The U.S. Department of Housing and Urban Development (HUD), which enforces the act, estimates that these design features add about 1 percent to construction costs. According to Robert Sheehan, an economist for the National Apartment Association, Washington, DC, the FHAA will add about $600 to the estimated $60,000 cost to construct each unit in a high-rise apartment building. That would translate into a monthly rental rise of some $5 to $7.[6]

With respect to existing multifamily housing, occupants with disabilities must be permitted to make alterations they need in order to use the unit. They may, for example, install grab bars in the bathroom or erect a ramp leading to an entry door. The law provides that the occupant is responsible for the costs of these alterations, just as all occupants pay for their own decorating and related expenses. The act allows landlords also to collect reimbursement for costs to restore the unit. However, there is no requirement that landlords make existing housing facilities accessible. (Some state laws require building owners to make "reasonable accommodations" in existing structures.)

The FHAA forbids discrimination on the basis of disability by real estate brokers, landlords, and others involved in sale and rental estate. Landlords and brokers may not inquire about a person's disability. Rather, the decision to rent or not to rent to an applicant must be based on universal criteria such as ability to pay. Owners may not falsely state that a unit is not available. Land-lords may not refuse to rent an apartment to a qualified applicant who has a disability. Real estate brokers may not steer applicants toward, or away from, any house, building or complex on the basis of disability. Charging more for rental or leased units, just because an applicant or tenant is disabled, is also discriminatory.

This provision banning discrimination by landlords and realtors, although it has little if any financial impact, may prove to be the most difficult part of the FHAA to implement. Patricia Moore, executive director of the Long Island Center for Independent Living, states that "steering" by realtors is common in New York. She adds that it may be necessary for undercover investigators to "fake" disability while pretending to apply for apartments in order to demonstrate just how widespread such discrimination is.[7]

Individuals with disabilities who believe they have been discriminated against contrary to the intent of the act may file complaints with the department. Such complaints must be submitted within one year of the alleged act of discrimination. The Secretary of Housing and

Contrary to what you might think, the number
of Americans with disabilities is increasing.

Many veterans, including these
Vietnam vets, have disabilities.

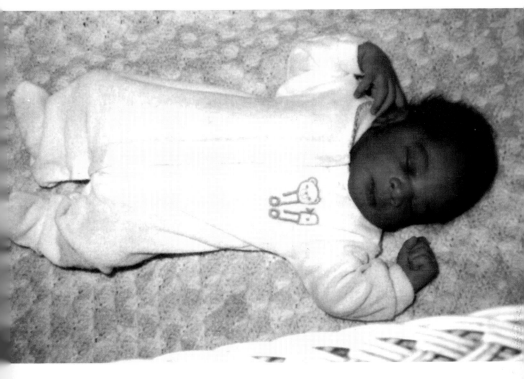

A normal-weight baby (above) and
a premature baby. Babies born to
drug-addicted mothers are often premature.

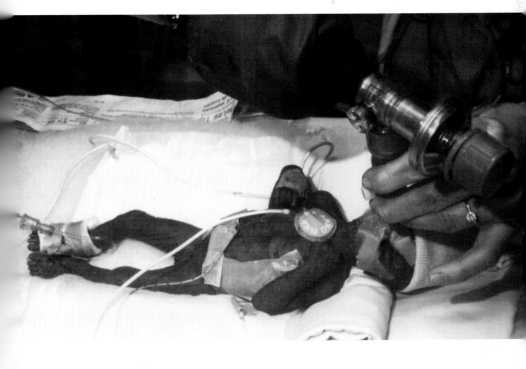

A curb specially designed
for wheelchair use

Sign language facilitates
communication in the classroom.

Most elementary school
students with disabilities
attend regular schools.

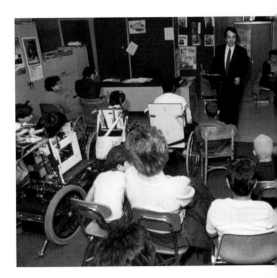

Most secondary school students
with disabilities also
attend regular schools.

This college student,
who is blind, is taking
notes in Braille.

Vans can be specially equipped so that people with certain physical disabilities can drive.

Public buses equipped with wheelchair lifts such as this one are still small in number.

Above: Some subway and light-rail stations have ramps for people using wheelchairs.

Right: The Americans with Disabilities Act is expected to change many things for the disabled.

# For millions of people, this is their first bus pass.

The Americans With
Disabilities Act

Public Law 101-336

Before the Americans with Disabilities Act, few public buses were
wheelchair accessible. But now that it's law, millions of Americans are finally
receiving their long awaited, and much deserved, ticket to ride.

**Because public transportation is for everyone.**

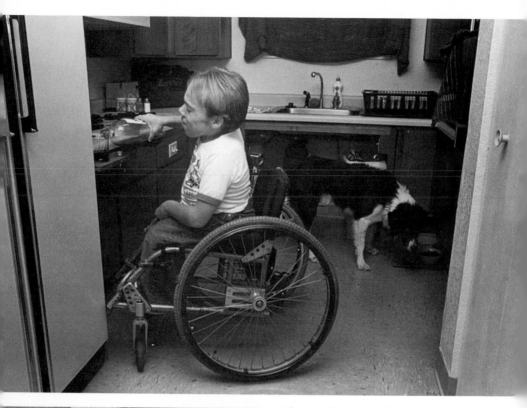

Above: This man lives in an apartment complex specially designed for people with disabilities. Notice that his kitchen counters are, at wheelchair level, easily accessible.

Left: This elevator has buttons in Braille for use by people who are blind.

Group homes provide a living situation for many people who are mentally ill or retarded.

New home fittings such as this kitchen faucet are attractive and easily used by everyone—young and old, disabled or nondisabled, strong or weak.

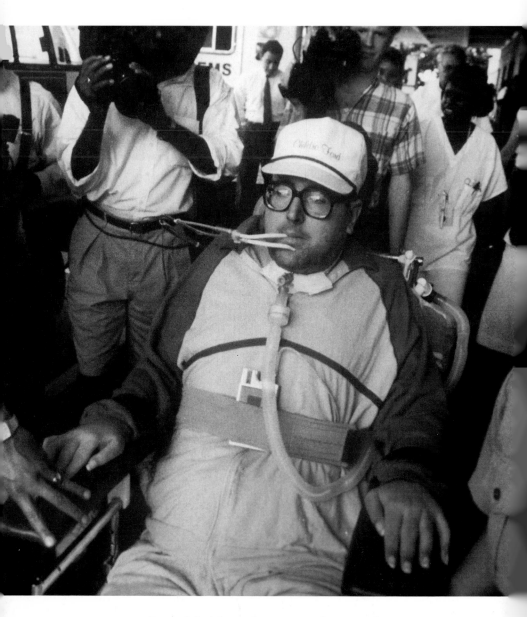

Larry McAfee, who attracted national
attention in 1990 by seeking court
permission to commit suicide

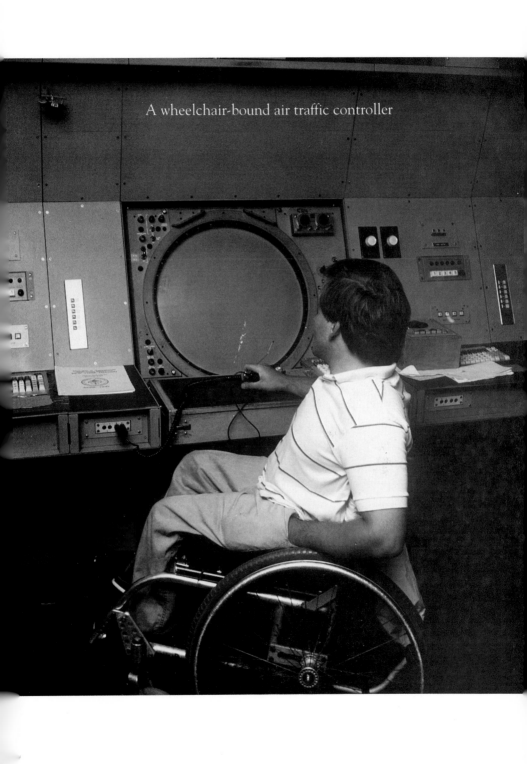

A wheelchair-bound air traffic controller

People with disabilities can do almost anything for a living, from assembling VCRs, to answering phones, to tuning pianos, to coaching basketball, to taking photographs.

Left: Telecommunication Devices for the Deaf makes phone conversations possible for people who are deaf, severely hearing impaired, or speech impaired.

Below: A closed-caption device enables people who can't hear or who hear poorly to understand television programs.

Above: In 1990, President Bush signed
the Americans with Disabilities Act.
Below: Peter Bonavita, who has
Lou Gehrig's disease, "speaks" by
blinking his eyes. A computer translates
the blinks, letter by letter, into words.

Left: Pop singer Stevie Wonder demonstrates a voice synthesis system that can be used by blind people to write music.

Below: The robotic arm delivers a computer disk to this woman, who is unable to reach the disk by herself. Do all Americans with disabilities have a right to adaptive technologies to help them in their daily lives?

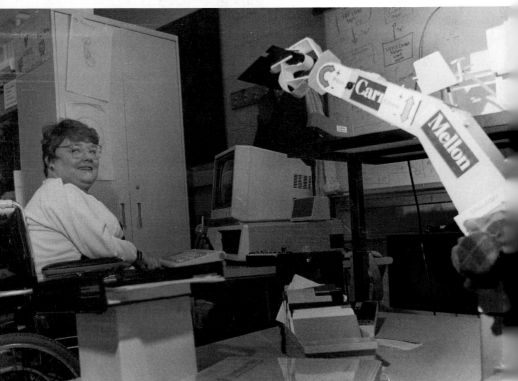

Urban Development may also file complaints. The act authorizes penalties against building owners of up to $10,000 for the first offense, $25,000 for the second offense, and $50,000 for the third.

The attorney general and the U.S. Department of Justice may bring "pattern and practice" cases against complex and building owners who repeatedly violate the act. In such cases, a district court may award penalties as high as $50,000 for a first offense and $100,000 for any subsequent violation. Individuals with disabilities who incur attorneys' fees in bringing discrimination complaints may receive reimbursement for those expenses.

If an individual files a complaint with HUD and does not receive satisfactory resolution, he or she may file suit in a federal district court at any time up to two years following the date of alleged discrimination. Actual and punitive damages may be awarded in such cases. The court may also issue injunctions and restraining orders. Again, attorneys' fees may be awarded.

## Group Homes

If anything, housing for mentally ill/emotionally disturbed persons is even less available than is housing for people with physical disabilities. Hundreds of thousands of adults with mental illness were dumped from state hospitals in the late 1970s and during the 1980s. State governments promised to provide "group homes," or supervised private houses, for the deinstitutionalized patients. Up to twelve adults live with six supervisors in a typical group home, such as the one on Pearl Street in New York's North Lawrence. "The house gives them camaraderie and friendship. If they're not feeling too good, they have a staff there to talk to," says Karen Mankin, a mental health specialist.[8]

In most states, however, few such homes were built, largely because of community opposition. Communities resist group homes out of a misguided belief that accepting them will lower property values; the experience of New York and other states having many group homes is that no such devaluation of property occurs.[9] Another reason for opposition is that some group-home residents are mentally restored (formerly mentally ill) individuals. Today, former mental patients make up very large proportions, by some estimates as many as half, of all homeless Americans. Although group homes are a well-established alternative to homelessness on the one hand and institutionalization on the other, most states have yet to create such homes.

There are other problems. Pay for group-home counselors is far below that for hospital workers with similar duties. And there are nowhere near enough homes. New York, with 204 group homes for mentally ill adults, is a national leader, but even it needs many more homes than community support allows it to buy. In New York, thousands of mentally ill people wait six to ten *years* for placement in a group home. Nassau County Commissioner of Mental Health Isadore Shapiro estimates that 500 mentally ill people are awaiting group-home placement in his county alone.[10] That's because Long Island's three psychiatric facilities (Central Islip, Kings Park, and Pilgrim Psychiatric) house just 5,000 patients today, down from 34,000 in 1960.[11]

Community opposition against people who are mentally ill continues to stall group-home development. A 1991 national survey of American adults found them significantly more uncomfortable with mentally ill persons than with any other group of people with disabilities. Just 19 percent of eighteen-or-older adults said they were comfortable with mentally ill individuals.[12]

Group homes for mentally retarded individuals have been accepted more readily by community members. The 1991 poll shows that 33 percent of American adults feel "very comfortable" with people who are retarded. That's particularly true in the six states which have half of all group homes nationwide: Michigan, New York, Nebraska, California, Washington, and Minnesota.

The differences living outside institutions make is nothing short of remarkable.[13] A generation ago, nearly 200,000 retarded adults lived in unspeakable conditions in huge institutions such as New York's Willowbrook and Pennsylvania's Pennhurst. Warehoused in poor sanitary conditions, ill-fed, and neglected or drugged most of the day for reasons of "control," they often died in their early twenties. The development of group homes has more than halved the institution population to under 100,000.[14] Today, living in group homes, retarded adults are working full-time in places like McDonald's, community hospitals, and university cafeterias. And their life expectancies are approaching the national average.[15]

Today, living arrangements for mentally ill or mentally retarded people form a continuum. From most to least restrictive, the options are: state institution, private institution, nursing home, community intermediate care facility [ICF/MR], semiindependent living programs or supportive apartments, and independent living. In this continuum, group homes are in the "supportive apartments" category. Although it is as "least restrictive" an environment as many retarded or mentally ill people can live in, the supply of group homes remains far short of the need. Some estimates suggest that 60,000 retarded adults and several hundred thousand mentally ill adults nationwide are awaiting placement in group homes.[16,17]

Some two million retarded individuals continue living at home with their parents. In Philadelphia, parents still caring for adult children who are retarded sued the state for financial support. Noting that the state would have paid for therapy, food, attendant care, and other services in an institution or group home, David and Leona Fialkowski asked Pennsylvania why it should deny state support just because their son David, twenty-three, lives at home.[18]

The federal government has granted "waivers" to some forty states, allowing Medicaid-reimbursed services to be paid when a person with a disability lives at home.[19] New York received such a waiver in August 1991, after eight years of lobbying the federal Department of Health and Human Services.

## Federal Housing Programs

The major federal housing programs for people with disabilities before the FHAA were section 202 and section 8, both of the Housing Act of 1959, as amended. Section 202 supports construction of housing projects, public buildings designed for occupancy by elderly and disabled persons. Funds for the program have been so limited that six- or even ten-year waiting lists are common in many parts of the country, despite the fact that federally subsidized housing projects often are not safe and desirable places to live. The only nonelderly Americans with disabilities who qualify to live in section 202 projects are those with below-poverty incomes, usually those who are on Supplemental Security Income (SSI) welfare aid rolls.

Section 8 rent subsidies offer these poor persons with disabilities partial rent so that no more than a set percentage of their monthly incomes go for rent. Individuals who are on SSI usually qualify for the subsidies. However, because many landlords refuse to accept section 8 rent subsidies, because funds for the program are few, and because only a small proportion of Americans with disabilities get SSI benefits, the program has had only a limited effect in resolving the desperate shortage of accessible, affordable housing in America.

Until recently, only section 202 housing was required to be accessible to people with disabilities. The few exceptions were privately constructed apartments in those handful of states with accessible housing laws. The fact that some 99 percent of America's housing stock remained inaccessible as late as 1990 has had devastating effects on the lives of people with disabilities. Many felt they had to give up on their dreams of an independent life-style, withdraw from the labor force, and live on very low incomes so as to qualify for SSI and thereby become eligible for accessible housing.

Section 202 housing is public "project" housing, and as such it suffers from many of the same problems public housing projects everywhere exhibit: poor maintenance, widespread drug abuse, and the stigma of living in segregated housing set aside for the poor. Since section 8 rent subsidies usually are applicable only at section 202 projects, the result is yet more segregation for people with disabilities.

## Simple Solutions

Although no law requires private one- or two-family homes to be accessible, a new concept in housing, called "universal design," is becoming popular. In part, that's due to the aging of the American population. Universal design combines accessibility for elderly and disabled people with ease-of-use for others.

American Standard, one of the nation's largest home fittings makers, has an entire line, called Heritage, of universal-design products. Gary Uhl, fittings product manager for American Standard, says: "The challenge was to replace the stigma of tasteless functionality with designs that appeal to all users.[20] For example, faucets have levers that require no twisting or turning to control water flow; traditional knobs had to be both gripped and twisted. Lumex makes tub guards and hairbrushes that are easier to grasp than are traditional devices. Bathtub grab bars now come in thirty-six colors, making them more aesthetic.

Lamps and other electricity-operated devices such as TVs or radios now can be turned on and off by clapping hands. Cellular phones can eliminate rushing to answer a ringing phone. Remote controls for many household appliances eliminate much extraneous movement.

Other "accessibility" products are also conveniences for people with no disabilities. Aiphone Communications Systems, for example, offers a product replacing a doorbell. An infrared camera installed where the doorbell usually is produces a video image of the visitor that is transmitted to a screen on a nightstand or on a wall. The door is unlocked if the home owner pushes a button.[21]

Not so simple to solve will be the problem of affordability. A survey of 1,400 disabled adults on Long Island, for example, found that the vast majority identified affordability of housing as a problem even greater than that of accessibility. The typical respondent reported an annual income of only $5,000. In an area where apartment rents average $860 per month, they would need twice that much just to pay the rent — with nothing left over for food, clothing, or other necessities.[22]

It will take years for the new nondiscrimination laws to take effect, allowing adults with disabilities to earn a living at jobs that pay enough to permit them to rent or purchase housing. Thus, long after the physical barriers fall in the face of the FHAA, the question will remain: "How can we make housing more affordable?" There are, unfortunately, no easy answers to that question.

Charles Carr, executive director of the Northeast Independent Living Program, in Lawrence, Massachusetts, is setting an example. His organization recently completed eight homes as part of a sixteen-unit project. The homes are designed to be both accessible and affordable. The need in the northern Massachusetts area for such housing is enormous, as it is nationwide. Sixteen homes will only make a dent in the overall problem. Carr notes, however, that it took eight years of planning to obtain the necessary permits and financing to construct even these few homes. The effort is worth it, he says, pointing out that it costs less than half as much for someone to live in a private home as it does to live in an institution. But economics is not the whole story. "It's a matter of dignity, too," Carr says.[23]

# EQUAL RIGHTS IN THE WORKPLACE

**"Not** working is perhaps the truest definition of what it means to be disabled."[1]

In the summer of 1990, a thirty-four-year-old civil engineer from Sanderson, Georgia, Larry McAfee, attracted national attention by seeking court permission to commit suicide. McAfee had been severely injured by a 1985 motorcycle accident that left him unable to move his arms or legs. After he learned how he could work despite these disabilities, he changed his mind about suicide. That fall, he secured a job with a company that designs computerized maps. The difference, McAfee says, is that the job gives him a future — something to live for.[2]

Working-age (16–64) adults with disabilities like McAfee number more than thirteen million.[3] But only four million work.

Most working-age adults with disabilities are "out of the labor force," that is, neither working nor actively seeking employment. That 68 percent of working-age adults with disabilities are not in the labor force is remarkable. Of nondisabled adults in the same age range, just 21 percent are out of the labor force. Most are voluntary nonparticipants: mothers of young children, full-time students, early-retired individuals, etc.

**TABLE 2**
**Labor Force Participation: Disabled and Nondisabled Adults Aged 16–64**

| Status | Disabled | Nondisabled |
|--------|----------|-------------|
| All | 100.0% | 100.0% |
| In the Labor Force | 31.6 | 78.9 |
| Out of the Labor Force | 68.4 | 21.1 |

These nine million adults with disabilities are out of the labor force because of discrimination in the workplace, because of undereducation, or because their disabilities are so severe that they cannot work.

Table 2 illustrates employment patterns as of 1989, the most recent year complete figures are available.[3]

### New Rights

Adults with disabilities only very recently have enjoyed rights in employment. Dating from 1976, federal agencies have given applicants and employees with disabilities equal opportunity in hiring and advancement decisions. Similar protection at large corporations — the 50,000 American firms that do contract work for federal agencies — also began in 1976. The Rehabilitation Act of 1973 requires such steps. In recent years, however, federal employment has leveled off at about three million civilian workers — and employment in big corporations actually fell by several million workers in the 1980s.

Most of the estimated fourteen million new jobs created in America since 1983 have been in smaller private companies, firms that rarely do government contract work.[4] This means that jobseekers with disabilities have not been protected against unjust discrimination on the basis of disability in the very companies doing most of the hiring in the decade just past. That lack of equal opportunity is an important reason for the dismal record of employment among American adults with disabilities.

The Americans with Disabilities Act addresses this problem. Subject to its provisions are virtually all companies with fifteen or more workers. The ADA requires private firms with twenty-five or more workers to offer jobseekers and employees with disabilities nondiscriminatory treatment in hiring and advancement as of July 26, 1992. Two years later, in 1994, the floor drops to fifteen or more workers. The ADA's mandates are similar to those provided for members of racial and ethnic minority groups in the 1964 Civil Rights Act. It took Congress twenty-six years to extend those protections to people with disabilities.[5]

## Americans with Disabilities Act

The ADA requires major changes in the way many companies do business. They must begin to actively recruit persons with disabilities, something few ever have done. For example, magazine advertisements picturing "typical" employees must include at least some persons who are visibly disabled. The rooms in which job applicants are interviewed and tested must be accessible to individuals using wheelchairs, crutches, or other aids. Employment tests themselves may not unfairly discriminate against applicants with disabilities. For example, a test that asks employees to listen to a tape and write their responses may not be used to screen out a deaf person just because that applicant cannot hear the tape. These are rather obvious "fair employment" measures, but they will be new to many companies. That's why the U.S. Equal Employment Opportunity Commission, the federal agency charged with enforcing the ADA's employment provisions, expects in 1993 alone to receive as many as 15,000 complaints alleging discrimination on the basis of disability.

The 1964 Civil Rights Act was amended in late 1991. The changes mean that disabled individuals who prove discrimination under the ADA are entitled to recover damages. There were no damage award provisions in the ADA when it was passed in 1990. However, the act did say that the remedies available under the 1964 act apply to ADA employment cases. The 1991 law provides a cap of $50,000 in damages where the employer is a small one; the cap rises to a maximum of $300,000 against large companies.

The ADA bans preemployment inquiries about disability: that is, an applicant may not be forced to admit that he or she has a disability. Any medical examination or other investigation may be performed only after a conditional job offer has been made; the purpose of this delay is to ensure that the employment decision is based on the individual's abilities and training, not on the disability. Employees are to be given "reasonable accommodations" needed to assist them in doing jobs for which they are qualified. As an example, a desk may be raised so that someone using a wheelchair can work there. A "reasonable" accommodation is one that does not impose an "undue hardship" on the employer.

The act also forbids employers to pay workers with disabilities less than nondisabled employees in the same jobs. Outlawed, too, are less than equal benefits, such as life or health insurance coverage. The act says that employees with disabilities are to be given the same health and other insurance as are workers with no disabilities; insurers are, however, permitted to decline to cover preexisting conditions if that policy is applied to all covered workers. Employees with disabilities must receive comparable education and training opportunities, and be able to participate in other employer-sponsored activities.

Under the ADA, employers may not assign individuals with disabilities to stereotyped jobs. One large photographic services company, for example, hired many blind individuals but assigned virtually all of them to positions in dark rooms. Another company had what it considered to be a "proud record" of employing deaf people, but put them to work operating noisy printing equipment. The act expressly forbids such disability-based job assignment. Employers now must allow individuals with disabilities to compete for jobs their abilities qualify them to perform. Jobseekers with disabilities undoubtedly will continue to be faced with stereotyping, but now they have legal recourse against unfair treatment.

Similarly, many companies that did hire people with disabilities in past years failed to allow these workers to advance in the business. The ADA specifically forbids discrimination on the basis of disability in promotions.

As powerful as it is, the ADA will not change attitudes overnight. Advocates worry that the EEOC is unlikely to "get tough" with small employers. Only time will tell us if the sweeping changes promised by the act lead to real changes in the workplace.

### Unemployment Rates

Among both men and women with disabilities, 14 percent of those in the labor force are unemployed.[3] The comparable rates among nondisabled men and women are in the 5- to 6-percent range. Thus, the unemployment rates for disabled adults are about double to triple those for nondisabled persons. In time, the ADA may lead to reduction in these high rates of unemployment.

The unemployment rate is a widely misunderstood proportion. The numerator comprises the number of individuals who are unemployed: in the denominator are persons working plus persons unemployed. An important point is that there is no place in the formula for people who are not in the labor force.

What does the 14 percent unemployment rate

among adults with disabilities tell us? It is a measure of how difficult it is for people actively seeking work to find it. The out-of-the-labor-force figure (68 percent), by contrast, talks about people who are not actively seeking work, either because they think they can't work or because they have been so frustrated in their employment that they have given up and dropped out.

## Occupation

Of the more than four million American adults with disabilities who do work, what kinds of jobs do they hold? That is a question of "occupational category." The most recent evidence from the U.S. Bureau of the Census is that people with disabilities hold many of the same kinds of jobs as do people without disabilities. This is illustrated in Table 3.

That so many disabled adults report only a high-school education suggests that many who work have blue-collar jobs. That is true. Adults with disabilities who work are more likely than are nondisabled persons to have laborer and machine-operative jobs, more likely to have service jobs, and more likely to be self-employed. They are, by contrast, less likely to hold managerial/professional jobs and less likely to work in retail trade, as Table 3 illustrates.

## Women with Disabilities

Only 27 percent of disabled women participate in the labor force, compared to 70 percent of nondisabled women. Three disabled women out of every four do not work.[3]

One reason is undereducation. While 21 percent of nondisabled working-age women have college degrees, that is true of only 7.5 percent of disabled women, or just one-third as many.

## TABLE 3
## Occupational Category: Disabled and Nondisabled
## Workers Aged 16–64

| | Males | | Females | |
|---|---|---|---|---|
| Occupation | Disabled | Non-disabled | Disabled | Non-disabled |
| Managerial/ Professional | 18.2% | 26.3% | 16.1% | 25.7% |
| Technical/ Sales/Clerical | 17.5 | 19.9 | 39.6 | 45.4 |
| Service | 12.5 | 9.2 | 27.3 | 17.1 |
| Farm/Forestry/ Fishing | 4.6 | 3.7 | 1.4 | 0.8 |
| Precision/Craft/ Production/Repair | 19.6 | 19.8 | 2.2 | 2.3 |
| Operator/ Fabricator/Repair | 27.4 | 20.9 | 13.4 | 8.7 |

## African-Americans with Disabilities

Two and one-half million African-American adults of
working age have disabilities. Only 22 percent of them
participate in the labor force, compared with 79 percent
of nondisabled black adults. In fact, disabled blacks made
up 35 percent of all black adults not in the labor force.[3]

Again, undereducation is an important reason. Just
6 percent of disabled black adults are college graduates,
as against 16 percent of nondisabled black adults.

## Hispanic-Americans with Disabilities

Just over one million working-age adults of Hispanic origin have disabilities. They are one out of every twelve
Hispanic adults. Only 23 percent of disabled Hispanic

adults participate in the labor force, compared with 74 percent of nondisabled Hispanic adults.[3]

Yet again, undereducation is an important factor. One in every four disabled adults of Hispanic origin never completed eighth grade. Just 7 percent are college graduates, vs. 14 percent of nondisabled adults of Hispanic origin.

## Training

Rules prohibiting discrimination, such as those implementing the Americans with Disabilities Act, are not enough. Jobseekers need to obtain the training needed to qualify for jobs. The EEOC explains: "While the ADA focuses on eradicating barriers, the ADA does not relieve a disabled employee or applicant from the obligation to perform the essential functions of the job. To the contrary, the ADA is intended to enable disabled persons to compete in the workplace based on the same performance standards and requirements that employers expect of persons who are not disabled."[6] That is, individuals with disabilities must compete with nondisabled persons for employment.

There are no goals or timetables in any disability employment laws. No preferences exist; no quotas are established. The obligation is upon the individual with a disability to secure the education and job training necessary to perform the job.

It will take time for the nation's nine million adults with disabilities who are not working to equip themselves for competitive employment. At least now, federal law assures these adults that the effort will be worthwhile. The time and money they put into job training will be investments in a productive future because no longer may employers bar them for non-job-related reasons.

Already, we are seeing changes. There are newspaper editors who are deaf, and magazine writers who are blind. There are air traffic controllers working at airports whose quadriplegia limits voluntary control of arm and leg muscles. There are comedians with cerebral palsy, network TV actors with Down syndrome, and rap singers who use motorized wheelchairs. The ADA will spur integration of people with disabilities into more "nontraditional" jobs, as people follow their dreams.

## Unmet Needs

The chairman of the EEOC, Evan Kemp, uses an electric wheelchair due to his physical disability. In summer 1991, Mr. Kemp testified to Congress that he would not be able to do that job without a "personal care attendant" (PCA) who helps him dress and eat at home. Since his appointment in 1989, Mr. Kemp has paid the attendant himself. In his testimony, however, he suggested that the federal agency he heads pay the attendant's salary as a "reasonable accommodation" to his disability.[7] Georgia's Larry McAfee has made a similar request. At present, no federal law interprets the term "reasonable accommodation" to require personal care attendants. Under current law it may be reasonable, however, for an employer to pay the salary of a sign-language interpreter who translates for a deaf worker on the job, or of a reader who reads written material out loud for a blind person. Extending the requirement on employers to off-the-job needs for personal assistance is perhaps the next step in the long road toward equal employment opportunity for all persons with disabilities.[8]

The debate over personal care attendant expenses illustrates some of the questions raised by enactment of the ADA. What is fair, both for jobseekers with disabilities and for employers? On the one hand, many severely physically disabled jobseekers could work full time if they had PCA assistance at home to help them to dress for and get to work. This argument is strikingly similar to that made by many working mothers that their employers should provide day-care services for young children. On the other hand, employers traditionally have viewed such off-the-job needs as personal concerns. Companies rarely pay workers' commuting costs, for example. Are the needs of physically disabled persons for assistance with at-home functions comparable to the needs of working mothers for assistance with their children? If so, are employer obligations comparable as well?

Another issue is raised by the nondiscrimination character of the ADA. Members of certain ethnic and racial minority groups benefit from federal affirmative action rules requiring that numerical goals and timetables be met. The ADA has no such requirements. Some advocates, pointing to the use of quotas in Europe and Japan, argue that numerical goals are appropriate as a means to make up for past discrimination on the basis of disability. Other advocates counter that the widespread public support of equal opportunity for people with disabilities might be undercut by a move toward quotas.

# EQUAL RIGHTS IN DAILY LIFE

"**O**n June 16, 1989, in Denver, Colorado, six wheelchair users entered a restaurant to eat lunch. They were told by the manager that they took up too much space, and unless they could get out of their wheelchairs and sit in regular seats, they would have to take their food out, or eat elsewhere. When they declined, the police were called. They were arrested and taken to jail. The arresting officer explained to them that if they had been asked to leave because they were black, the law would protect them, but that there was no law protecting persons with disabilities in this situation."

"'**I** had been a CPA [certified public accountant] and was a producer and director for CNN [Cable News Network] and PBS [Public Broadcasting System] up until the accident, June, 1987. [She sustained a traumatic brain injury in that accident.] Now, nothing. Have attempted suicide three times. I know hundreds [like me]. Most of us tried, but which way and where do we go? Where can we live? What and who can we be? If I were understood, cared for, educated for a new life and career, I would have something to live for.'"

" **A** deaf woman in constant pain from terminal cancer was admitted to one of the nation's most prestigious hospitals for major surgery. Unable to communicate because there were no interpreter services, she was denied timely services and forced to undergo unnecessarily painful and often inappropriate treatment without consultation or explanation."

" **A** 56-year-old father of three in Alabama, a former army captain with a graduate degree in business and education, was diagnosed with depression and anxiety at age 31. When this became known, his 16-year army, reserve and national guard career was terminated with no benefits. Although successful in business, he was fired three times when it was determined that he had a mental illness. He has lost his family and all his — possessions."[1]

●●●●●●●●●●●●●●●●●●●●●●●●●●●●●●●●●●●●●●●●●●●●●

Ironically, federal law left until last the part of life most of us take for granted — our daily lives as members of a community. It was not until 1992 that discrimination on the basis of disability in stores, restaurants, movie theaters, laundry establishments, and the like was outlawed in America.

As the examples quoted above illustrate, such discrimination is diverse and widespread. Remarkably, a full generation after federal law required that schools become accessible, so that children with disabilities could receive elementary and secondary education alongside nondisabled children, restaurants from coast to coast remained inaccessible for people using wheelchairs. Similarly, most Americans take for granted that when they go to a hospital, they'll be advised of their rights and of their options for surgery or other medical intervention. Deaf people, however, have rarely been offered such basic courtesies. While the ADA was being debated in Washington, Congress heard testimony that a teenage girl was refused entry into a movie theater because the theater owner feared she might upset his other customers. She now has the right to go to that theater.

## Places of Public Accommodation

Perhaps no other part of the landmark Americans with Disabilities Act will touch as many lives as will title III. This section of the ADA requires accessibility in what it calls "places of public accommodation." These include stores and shopping malls, hotels and motels, restaurants, movie theaters, recreation parks, museums, doctors' and lawyers' offices, banks, bowling alleys, health spas, laundromats, barbershops, and sports stadiums.

These are required to be accessible to and usable by individuals with disabilities. The effective date was January 26, 1992. Only a few exceptions apply. If the cost to remove a barrier is so excessive as to qualify as an "undue burden," the store or other place of public accommodation is excused from removing it; even then, however, the service provider must find some alternative way of providing "full and equal enjoyment" for customers, clients, or patients with disabilities. Elevators need not be installed in buildings with fewer than three floors or less than 3,000 square feet of space per floor.[2]

Most changes will be modest — and inexpensive. In stores, for example, clerks are now required to write on a pad for a deaf customer and to read price tags out loud for blind patrons. Neither accommodation costs anything. Shelves and displays in grocery and bookstores may need to be rearranged so as to facilitate movement of a customer using a wheelchair. Hotels must install flashing lights where auditory fire or other alarm signals are provided. Some paper towel dispensers in bathrooms must be lowered so that people using wheelchairs can reach them. Car rental agencies must offer at least a few cars that have hand controls.[3]

Although the changes may appear simple, they will enhance greatly the accessibility of communities in which people with disabilities live. For many, ADA's title III will open the door to an active community life. A 1986 Harris poll found that adults with disabilities on average saw just two theatrical films and attended only one sporting event a year. Similarly, many reported great problems doing daily shopping, banking, and other errands.[4] In time, title III of the ADA will reduce or eliminate these barriers, allowing people with disabilities to live fuller, more rewarding lives.

Many hundreds of thousands of small changes will be made, in communities across the country. Most will cost very little. The effect, however, will be cumulative. Many individuals with disabilities will be able to do their own shopping, for the first time. People using wheelchairs will be able to get into a barbershop as easily as they now can enter most libraries. They'll be able to use automatic teller machines at their local bank branch, again for the first time in their lives. A deaf person will see, upon entering a restaurant, a list of the "specials of the day."

## Telephones

About 93 percent of all American homes have telephones. Modern life, in fact, is unimaginable without the phone. Yet until just twenty-five years ago, deaf people were unable to use it — at all. Then a deaf scientist invented a device that used typing and reading in place of talking and listening. This "teletypewriter," now a small electronic "telecommunications device for the deaf" (TDD), allows two TDD users to "talk" to each other over the phone lines as easily as two hearing people do. That was quite enough for many deaf people who never before had made or received a single phone call. The next step, of course, was to extend the TDD's reach to include homes and businesses not equipped with TDDs.

Title IV of the Americans with Disabilities Act requires telephone companies to sponsor what are called "dual party relay services" that permit hearing- and/or speech-impaired people to gain equal access to telephone networks. In a relay, a telephone operator listens to what one person says and types those words for another individual to read. Such relays must be in place in all fifty states no later than July 1993. With them, a deaf person using a TDD can call, and be called by, anyone in the nation.

For the first time, many deaf, severely hearing impaired and speech impaired people can call to have a pizza delivered to the home. They can call bosses and coworkers, friends and relatives, and local movie theaters with equal ease.

### Television

Is there a right to understand TV? In 1990, the U.S. Congress decided that there was. It enacted a law requiring that as of July 1993, all thirteen-inch or larger (measured diagonally) television sets made or sold in America must be equipped with a "caption chip" making them capable of receiving and displaying captions, or subtitles, so that people who are deaf can understand what is said. That same year, Congress told the U.S. Department of Education to experiment with ways to make TV more accessible to blind people.

The idea that our national legislature has to act to make something as common as television "accessible" to people with disabilities may strike most people as remarkable. Today, almost every American home has at least one set. Most Americans watch several hours of TV daily. Television is our major source of news. When war erupted in the Persian Gulf in early 1991, for example, many of us turned to television to find out what was happening.

## TV and Deaf People

Television began in America in the late 1940s. By the mid-1950s, virtually every American home had a TV. Yet it was not until 1980 that a machine came along that could make television understandable to America's two million deaf citizens. Called a "closed caption decoder," it sells for about $200. This "black box" receives the captions transmitted from network or cable broadcasters. Connected to a TV set by cables, the decoder displays these typed words on the bottom of the screen. The effect is much like watching a subtitled foreign-language movie: the viewer shifts his or her glance between the action portrayed on the TV screen and the four lines of dialogue printed on the bottom portion of the screen.

The decoder launched a major step forward for deaf people. As the decade of the 1980s unfolded, more and more network and cable programs were captioned. In 1990, for the first time, 100 percent of prime time (8:00–11:00 P.M.) network programs were captioned. Yet, due to the cost of the decoder and the difficulty of attaching it to the TV set, fewer than 10 percent of deaf Americans owned one. Since captioning each half hour of TV programming cost about $2,000, industry leaders were beginning to express reservations about continuing to pay for captions when so small a proportion of the audience used them. Said a spokesman for the American Broadcasting Company (ABC): "Increased decoder ownership — not just more captioning — is required for a strong, self-sustaining captioning service."[5] The National Captioning Institute (NCI), a private captioning organization, concurred: To make the captioned service economically viable and self-sustaining, captioning must reach into at least 500,000 homes and ideally 1,000,000 homes by 1990."[6] At the time, 1987, reaching that goal would mean tripling the number of decoders in fewer than three years.

What could accomplish so rapid a change? Congress decided in 1990 that television was so central to American life that it was in the national interest that TV be accessible to deaf people. It passed the Television Decoder Circuitry Act[7] in October of that year. The law requires that every thirteen-inch or larger TV set manufactured or sold in the United States after July 1, 1993, must have a built-in computer chip that does what the closed-caption decoder box does. That is, just as every TV set is capable of receiving network and local station broadcasts, so too must it be able to receive captions. Such caption-ready TV sets are the electronic equivalents of ramps and elevators in buildings.

The potential of such chips is compelling. Some fifteen to twenty million TV sets are sold in America each year. Thus, within one year of the introduction of caption-ready TV sets, the number of American homes capable of receiving captions will increase from a small fraction of one million to well over fifteen million. A market of that size will virtually guarantee that captioning will survive. Every dollar spent encoding captions for TV programming will deliver a vastly greater return on investment.

Congress was convinced that something else equally remarkable would happen once caption chips were inside every TV set. Just as mothers pushing baby strollers, delivery persons using dollies, bicycle riders, and others discovered the benefits of curb cuts once those were widely installed in the nation's streets, so too would families discover uses for captioning. Captions could provide important benefits for persons who are not hearing-impaired. Captions could, for example, help preschool children learn to read. They could help illiterate adults become literate. They could help foreign-language-speaking Americans acquire English. And they could help persons in other nations to learn English.

The television industry responded to this vision. Beginning in 1990, such TV manufacturers as Zenith, Sanyo, and Sony began making plans to build caption chips into their TVs. They reported that the cost of the chips likely would be as low as $5, so caption-capable TV sets probably would not cost much more than earlier sets. Zenith said that TVs equipped with the chip might appear in stores as early as 1992.[8] In fact, the first Zenith sets were sold in late 1991.

### TV and Blind People

The 1,700,000 Americans who are blind (20/200 vision, or worse) or have low vision (40/200 or "tunnel" vision) have a problem that is opposite to that of deaf Americans. While deaf people can see the action, but miss the dialogue, blind people hear what is said but do not see what happens on screen.

In 1989, a remarkable new technology appeared that seemed to promise help for blind people. The introduction of "stereo" TV in the mid-1980s, in which two audio tracks are provided, was spurred at first by MTV. Could stereo TV help blind people? Experts on blindness wondered if some way could be found to use the second audio track to carry what they called "descriptive video services." These are spoken words explaining what is happening on TV. For a show such as "Matlock," for example, the spoken dialogue would be carried by the first of the two audio tracks, but the second could explain what is happening in a car or while a crime is being committed.

This idea seemed to have a lot of merit. Blind people working as telephone company operators, for example, had shown that they were skilled in listening to a caller in one ear while, at the same time, hearing through the other ear a computer voice speaking out loud the contents of a telephone directory.

In 1990, Congress decided to see if stereo TV could be used in much the same way. In the Individuals with Disabilities Education Act,[9] it provided money to the U.S. Department of Education for use in demonstrating the potential of stereo TV for blind viewers. One public television station, WGBH-TV in Boston, was already planning such studies.

Descriptive video is not yet widely available on commercial television. However, if the experiments Congress has authorized prove that stereo TV promotes their understanding of television, it is possible that this new service may soon become as pervasive as captioning is today.

## Minimum Income

Because equal rights in education took effect as recently as 1977, and employment rights in private companies only in 1992, many adults with disabilities have no jobs and no realistic prospect of gainful employment. For these people, a 1974 federal law created Supplemental Security Income (SSI). This federal-state program provides a "guaranteed minimum income" for people with disabilities who otherwise could not afford food and housing.[10]

SSI is funded by thirteen billion in federal dollars, which are supplemented, often generously, by the states. Typical beneficiaries receive $400 each month from the federal government, although some states double that amount. In addition, people who get SSI often are eligible for food stamps as well. SSI recipients usually are covered by Medicaid, the $34 billion federal-state medical program for poor people.

These programs are controversial among people with disabilities. Some argue that SSI and Medicaid are, in effect, welfare "handouts" that people can get just by being disabled, without having to work for them. Individuals with disabilities who worked hard to get an education, and then worked even harder to get and keep a good job, sometimes resent the fact that others with the same kinds of disabilities can spend their days watching soap operas and still get enough money to pay the rent, buy food and clothing, and receive medical care. Seen in this light, SSI and Medicaid can rob people with disabilities of the incentives needed to become independent, self-supporting citizens.

Other advocates are angry because SSI and Medicaid have many outdated rules that make it difficult to get off these aid rolls and onto payrolls. Youths and adults with disabilities who benefit from SSI may lose eligibility if they engage in "substantial gainful activity" which usually means earning more than $500 a month. A 1986 amendment — section 1619 — to the Social Security Act allows some individuals to earn much more and yet keep Medicaid coverage. This program was designed to encourage SSI recipients to accept jobs paying more than the previously allowed amount.[10] Many advocates are concerned, however, that section 1619 doesn't go far enough. In fact, relatively few SSI recipients have left the Social Security rolls for payrolls under the section 1619 program.

SSI and Medicaid have helped some individuals to work, however. Severely disabled individuals living in group homes work full-time. Their SSI checks are signed over to the group home administrators to pay for room and board. SSI and Medicaid also help people with disabilities who have no alternative. All told, about three million disabled Americans receive SSI checks every month. Included are some 750,000 children under age eighteen who are both disabled and poor.[11] Many would not have enough to eat, or adequate health coverage, without SSI and Medicaid.

Three adults with disabilities in every ten have

below-poverty incomes. Among those living in families, the mean family income of below-poverty adults with disabilities was $6,197; among those living by themselves or with unrelated persons, the mean for persons with disabilities was just $3,218.[12] The monthly checks may be small, but the additional benefits that come with SSI eligibility, particularly Medicaid and food stamps, but also federal rent subsidies, are important.

On the other hand, SSI could offer an excuse not to work, an excuse that may be inappropriate now that strong federal laws prohibit discrimination in employment on the basis of disability. Such laws as the Americans with Disabilities Act, section 504, and others offer even very severely disabled individuals an opportunity to work to support themselves.

A 1986 survey by the Harris polling firm revealed that some two-thirds of all SSI recipients would be willing to leave the SSI rolls for payrolls if they were offered good jobs.[4] Perhaps now that the Americans with Disabilities Act is law, many will take a chance on employment.

# THE DISABILITY RIGHTS MOVEMENT

**"T**wo thousand letters were received which supported the Americans with Disabilities Act. There was one letter in opposition…. There were very few requests for maintenance welfare benefits. The vast majority of requests were for rights and services that would enable people to become active and productive participants in the mainstream of society. A strong work ethic was expressed."

**"H**owever, the job is not yet finished. I look forward to working with all of you to uphold the magnificent promise of ADA by ensuring that people with disabilities are full participants in the mainstream of American life."[1]

President George Bush, January 25, 1991

Of the estimated thirty-six to forty-three million Americans with disabilities, several hundred thousand are active in the disability rights movement. Their organized efforts pushed through the Americans with Disabilities Act (ADA) at a time of national conservatism and of retrenchment in civil rights generally. The Supreme Court had issued five rulings restricting the rights of minorities over the previous several years, none advancing them. Yet the ADA, widely called the most ambitious civil rights measure in twenty-five years, sailed through the U.S. House of Representatives 377–29 and the U.S. Senate 91–6. It was signed into law by President George Bush, whom liberals criticized for lacking a domestic agenda, at 10:26 A.M. on July 26, 1990.

The movement at the time was spearheaded by an ad hoc private sector group called the Task Force on the Rights and Empowerment of Americans with Disabilities. Appointed by U.S. Representative Major R. Owens (D-NY), chairman of the Select Education Subcommittee in the House, the thirty-eight-member task force was chaired by Justin Dart, Jr., a Republican from Texas. Dart, who had polio in the 1950s, and his colleagues on the task force served without pay, and paid their own travel and other expenses. Dart personally traveled to all fifty states, hosting sixty-three "public forums" attended by 7,000 people with disabilities and speaking to hundreds of conventions attended by more than 25,000 people. The task force collected 5,000 written examples of discrimination as evidence that the act was needed. Most members of the task force were themselves people with disabilities.

Although the task force was hugely successful, it was a temporary body. It voted to disband in October 1990, its work done.[1]

The disability movement has no umbrella group comparable to the National Organization for Women or the National Association for the Advancement of Colored People. There are several important national advocacy organizations, but these focus on particular topics or segments of the population. The Disability Rights Education and Defense Fund , with offices in Berkeley, California and Washington, DC, is one advocacy organization. Another is the Consortium for Citizens with

Disabilities, organized by several single-disability groups based in Washington, DC; both were active in the task force.

Most national advocacy is handled by disability-specific organizations. Among the more active are the United Cerebral Palsy Associations, Inc., Washington, DC; The Arc, formerly the Association for Retarded Citizens of the United States, Arlington, TX; National Easter Seals Society, Chicago, IL; American Council of the Blind, Washington, DC; National Council on Independent Living, Washington, DC; Self Help for Hard of Hearing People, Bethesda, MD; and National Association of the Deaf, Silver Spring, MD.

## Beginnings

The disability rights movement began at the University of Illinois and at the University of California at Berkeley in the 1960s as college students with physical disabilities sought to eliminate architectural and transportation barriers on and around college campuses. Their efforts led to the creation of the first of what are now more than 300 "centers for independent living" (CILs) in cities across the nation. Such pioneer centers as the Boston Center for Independent Living and the Center for Independent Living in Berkeley set the tone for the independent living movement. CILs "fight city hall" to get ramps installed in buildings, curb cuts made in sidewalks, and transportation and housing made accessible to local residents with disabilities.

Also in the late 1960s, organizations founded by parents of children with disabilities, among them the Association for Children and Adults with Learning Disabilities and the Association for Retarded Citizens of the United States, advocated for equal educational rights in the public schools. The Pennsylvania chapter of this second group, for example, led the fight in the landmark 1972 *PARC* v. *Pennsylvania* district court case that helped bring about what is now the Individuals with Disabilities Education Act.

In the early 1970s, returning veterans of the Vietnam era who had been disabled in that conflict joined with others with severe disabilities to create an umbrella organization, the American Coalition of Citizens with Disabilities (ACCD). It was no accident that veterans with spinal cord injuries emerged as movement leaders. They had vivid recollections of a freer, more mobile life, and anger at what they saw as the injustice of returning to an inaccessible America. The coalition was the first cross-disability advocacy organization in the United States.[2] Between 1975 and 1981, it led the movement for greatly expanded civil rights in education, transportation, housing, and other areas of daily life. The coalition folded in 1983, a victim of the 1981–1982 recession.

There are few recorded instances of civil rights advocacy among Americans with disabilities prior to the 1960s, in large part because advocacy requires that people have their own personal lives in control well enough to be able to look beyond their immediate personal needs. For most of America's two-hundred-plus years, such self-sufficiency has been impossible due to undereducation, community barriers, and widespread unemployment. As an example, the founding president of the American Coalition of Citizens with Disabilities worked in Chicago in the 1950s at a sheltered workshop for ten cents an hour. It was not until she got a job as a social worker in a New York City hospital that this blind woman was able to gain enough control over her daily life to begin local, then national, advocacy work.[3]

In the late 1700s and throughout most of the 1800s, American towns and states segregated people with disabilities into institutions. These were, almost without exception, located in remote rural areas, so as not to "offend the sensibilities" of the local populace. This was particularly true of people who were deaf, blind, mentally retarded or mentally ill. Americans with physical disabilities for the most part stayed at home, prisoners of inaccessible architecture. They literally could not get out and about in the community. These barriers would not begin to fall until the late 1970s.

It was not until then, after the minority group civil rights movement of the late 1950s and mid-1960s, that the ideas arose that persons with disabilities are minority group members and that society has some obligations to its disabled citizens. For the first time, parents went to court in the early 1970s, demanding that their children with disabilities have access to an education in the local public schools. That led, in 1975, to IDEA. At about the same time, the U.S. Congress passed the 1973 Rehabilitation Act, the final sentence of which was the nation's first-ever disability rights statute, section 504.

Suddenly, in the mid-1970s, America was saying that the country had obligations to do something to the environment, to society itself, in order to accommodate persons with disabilities. This is a far cry from the original approach of removing them from the populated towns and villages and placing them into warehousing institutions. Now society was saying that the streets, the libraries, the schools, and the places of work should be made accessible to, opened up to, people with disabilities. In large part, it was section 504 that did that: between 1977 and the late 1980s, section 504 led to the removal of architectural barriers in virtually every kind of government building and public facility.

The elimination of barriers, in turn, freed Americans with disabilities to advocate for yet more rights. To take just one example, task force chairman Justin Dart logged hundreds of thousands of miles in airplanes, trains, buses, and cars and spoke in hundreds of auditoriums, college classrooms, and libraries in all fifty states. Many of these facilities would not have been accessible to him just ten years earlier.[1]

## The Movement Today

In recent years, the disability rights movement has joined forces with organizations advocating for other disadvantaged minorities in America. The task force, for example, worked closely with the American Civil Liberties Union (ACLU) and with the Leadership Conference on Civil Rights (LCCR), an umbrella group of unions, churches, and civil rights organizations representing African-Americans, Hispanics, and women.

The joint efforts were begun in the late 1970s by the ACCD when it sought implementation of section 504. More recently, the ACLU and LCCR helped disability rights organizations to amend the Fair Housing Act (FHA) to include people with disabilities. The Fair Housing Amendments Act of 1988 could not have been enacted without the support of organizations representing the traditional beneficiaries of FHA legislation.

While it is branching out to enlist the support of "natural allies" from other movements, however, the disability rights movement faces a schism within its own ranks. Several million adults who receive monthly Social Security Disability Insurance (SSDI) and Supplemental Security Income (SSI) checks want to retain these benefits, which originally were provided because of the omnipresent barriers in American communities. Now that these barriers are gone or fast falling, some SSDI and SSI beneficiaries fear losing their government subsidies. Such fears are realistic at a time of massive federal deficits.

The schism illustrates a philosophical debate that continues to rage within the disability rights community. Some advocates look upon Denmark and Sweden as offering models for what America should do. In these Scandinavian countries, services and devices often are given without charge to people with disabilities, whether or not they work to support themselves. The model, these advocates say, is one of a liberal government reflecting a caring society that does what is needed to assure every citizen with a disability a life of health, security, and comfort.

Other advocates regard the Scandinavian approach as unacceptably paternalistic. These advocates believe that the role of government is not to provide handouts but rather to assure a fair chance at self-sufficiency. In their view, people with disabilities can only become independent if they work and use their pay to support themselves.

There are several divisions within the movement. While the ADA expressly recognizes, as individuals with disabilities, people disabled by the human immunodeficiency virus (HIV) that causes AIDS, not all adults with more traditional disabilities such as paraplegia or retardation are anxious to be identified with persons with AIDS. There is prejudice among disabled Americans toward people with AIDS just as there is among nondisabled Americans. Such prejudices were largely set aside in the fight for the ADA. Leaders of Paralyzed Veterans of America, for example, wheeled through the corridors of Congress carrying large signs proclaiming the need to end discrimination against people with AIDS. An individual with AIDS, David Bodenstein, served on the task force. He died of the disease just before the act was passed.[1]

Some debates are over tactics, not goals. One fast-rising organization in the disability rights movement is ADAPT. Originally formed to fight for accessible transportation (the acronym stood for Americans Disabled for Accessible Public Transportation), and now organized to advocate for personal care attendant services, ADAPT takes a militant approach to civil rights activism. In 1989, ADAPT members demonstrated for the ADA in Washington. Dozens were arrested, something they regarded as a point of pride. The following year, ADAPT disrupted rush-hour traffic outside the Social Security Administration's Baltimore headquarters in an effort to bring public attention to SSA's failure to provide PCA services. Again, many of its members were arrested. The Disability Rights Education and Defense Fund (DREDF), mentioned earlier, takes a more traditional approach. Rather than go to the streets to demonstrate, DREDF prefers to lobby the halls of Congress to get the votes needed to enact powerful new laws.

The tactical divisions occur even within single-disability communities. In blindness, for example, the Baltimore-based National Federation of the Blind (NFB) believes in public demonstrations and pickets to call attention to the needs of blind people. By contrast, the American Council of the Blind, based in Washington, takes the DREDF approach of quiet lobbying on Capitol Hill. The NFB's *Braille Monitor* magazine spends almost as much time criticizing the conservative council as it does arguing for more independence for blind Americans.

The movement is in some cases so splintered that it is a miracle that Congress and the White House can figure out what people with disabilities want and need. Take, for example, deafness. The 15,000-member National Association of the Deaf, headquartered in Silver Spring, Maryland, supposedly speaks for deaf people. But the Association of Late Deafened Adults, based in Chicago, represents people who lost their hearing later in life. The Oral Deaf Adults Section of the Washington-based Alexander Graham Bell Association for the Deaf speaks for deaf individuals who use speech and lipreading as their preferred means of communication. And Self Help for Hard of Hearing People (SHHH), based in Bethesda, Maryland, represents people who regard themselves as hard-of-hearing rather than as deaf. Quite often, they say very different things, as we shall see in the next chapter.

# WHAT IS NEXT?

**T**he landmark Americans with Disabilities Act is widely expected to make America a much more accessible nation by the mid- to late-1990s. Combined with the Fair Housing Amendments Act and other recent laws, it should greatly reduce discrimination in our country. Some students of disability in America might ask the question, "What is next?" As it happens, there's quite a bit left to be done, including finding answers to some difficult questions.

## Is There a Right to Technology?

Labor Day, 1991. Tens of millions of Americans watch as Peter Bonavita, forty-five, uses a computer to surmount the effects of amyotrophic lateral sclerosis (ALS), often called Lou Gehrig's disease. Bonavita "speaks" by blinking his eyes. A computer translates the blinks letter by letter into words, then speaks them out. Although it can take him five minutes to compose a sentence most people could speak in fifteen seconds, the machine is a breakthrough toward greater independence for the Vietnam veteran who contracted ALS twenty years ago. The former Nikon product manager also has a page-turning machine. Nineteen years ago, Bonavita was told he had two years to live. Today, even his doctors won't guess how much longer he has.[1]

Bonavita's story raises some important questions, most of them about money. The state of the art in adaptive technology has reached a remarkable level. Millions of Americans have seen Xerox commercials showing singer Stevie Wonder "reading" his mail using a Kurzweil Personal Reader that translates print into a computerized voice. The device costs $12,000. Other, less well-known products are equally as expensive. Dragon Systems, a Massachusetts voice recognition systems maker, offers Dragon Dictate, a computer product enabling people with quadriplegia and other severe mobility limitations to write entire manuals or books just by speaking into a microphone. The cost exceeds $10,000.

Other products are much less expensive. A Telecommunication Device for the Deaf (TDD) permitting an individual who cannot hear to use the telephone costs as little as $175. About thirty states distribute them free of charge to "certified" deaf, hard-of-hearing, and speech-impaired persons. "Talking" calculators and alarm clocks for blind individuals can be purchased for as little as $20. Controls for turning electrical appliances, ranging from room lights to TV sets, on or off just by clapping hands are even less expensive.

Of America's estimated thirty-six million people with disabilities, only a small minority owns such adaptive devices. The American Foundation for the Blind has estimated that no one product for blind people has helped even 5 percent of the population of blind and low-vision people.[2] Similarly, just 200,000 adults who are deaf own TDDs, about one in every ten who could use the machines.

Is there a "right" to adaptive technology? We as a nation have not yet answered that question. There is no discernible logic to the current system. Californians who are both deaf and blind are entitled to a $5,500 special TDD that prints out words in Braille, free of charge, but deaf-blind residents of New York must buy their own.

Residents of Massachusetts may receive, free, a $5 large-button overlay enabling someone with cerebral palsy to push telephone numbers accurately, but those living in Vermont may not. When it comes to $400 computer programs that permit a PC to "speak" or a $100 "keyguard" that helps people with fine motor control limitations to type on a keyboard, people in all fifty states must pay for them.

Such seeming irrationality — some states provide products free, others don't; some products are distributed to qualified persons while other products are not — appears tailor-made for conversion into a single federal program. Yet the only federal law fitting the bill, the Technology Related Assistance for Individuals with Disabilities Act of 1988, is funded at just $20 million — about 75 cents for each American with a disability!

At a time of federal and state budget deficits, can the nation afford to provide state-of-the-art devices to people with disabilities? Given that these products may permit them to work to support themselves, can the country afford *not* to?

### From Aid Rolls to Payrolls?

In America today, some eight million adults with disabilities receive federal and state welfare payments under the Supplemental Security Income (SSI) program, income replacement payments under the Social Security Disability Insurance (SSDI) program, and/or cash awards from state workers' compensation programs. The state workers' compensation programs date from 1911, SSDI from 1956, and SSI from 1974 — all prior to implementation of civil rights for people with disabilities. The federal government alone spends some $100 billion annually on SSDI and SSI, including Medicare and Medicaid coverage, for eight million disabled adults. The states add more than $25 billion in worker's compensation annually.[2]

When adults with disabilities work to support themselves instead of relying on government to support them, two things happen. First, they pay taxes on their income. And second, they no longer qualify for most federal and state subsidies. Savings to taxpayers are considerable. Were one million SSDI and Medicare recipients, for example, to work instead of drawing benefits, each of the nation's 115 million workers would save more than $100 a year in federal income taxes.

It is, of course, not that simple. To work, people with disabilities need a job, one for which they are qualified. They need a place to live, one accessible to them. They need transportation to and from work, as well as around the community. A decade ago, most of the estimated eight million aid beneficiaries with disabilities could not acquire any of these. Even today, a minority can put the pieces together. But within the next decade, housing, transportation, and employment should become much more readily available even to people with severe disabilities. At that point, the nation will need to decide if the time has come to insist that individuals with disabilities become self-supporting.

John Kemp, executive director of United Cerebral Palsy Associations Inc. (UCPA), for one, thinks that time may come. "It's up to us," he says. Kemp, a former Easter Seals poster boy, was born with no arms or legs. Using artificial limbs, he completed law school and has supported himself independently for twenty years.[3] He knows it is not realistic to expect everyone with a disability to do what he has done. But the day is fast coming when such goals probably should be set for most children and adults with disabilities.

### Excellence in Special Education?
That would mean providing children not just with access to an education, which is guaranteed today, but with a quality education that prepares them to support them-

selves. Will America extend its commitment to excellence in education to include children with disabilities? U.S. Department of Education assistant secretary Robert R. Davila, the nation's top special educator, believes that the goal is realistic but that important questions must be answered first. "What is a quality education?" asks Davila. "For a child who is seriously emotionally disturbed? For one who is profoundly retarded? Can we agree upon standards for measuring whether a school is giving them an education that is in fact 'excellent'?"[4]

Federal law in special education is based on the belief that integration of disabled and nondisabled children in public school classrooms is the ideal. That value judgment reflects the reality that the level of instruction offered in the average American classroom is higher than that provided in the average separate, "special" classroom. Yet, as suggested in chapter 4, this is not always true. For many children who are retarded, for example, a better education may be offered in a segregated setting where specially designed curricula meet the children's unique needs.

This may be a case where the values of mainstreaming and of excellence conflict. The conflict is sharply framed: To teach retarded children what they need to know, we should place them in separate classrooms. That means not integrating them in regular classrooms. We cannot do both. If we decide that quality is more important than integration for these children, we might have to change the landmark Individuals with Disabilities Education Act, which has a clear preference for education "in the least restrictive environment." Doing so, however, weakens that law, and in time might mean less integration, as well, for children with other disabilities.

That the task of offering disabled children a quality education may be difficult should not dissuade us from making the effort. The nation cannot be satisfied with the low average levels of achievement reported by the

U.S. Department of Education. The hard-won civil rights gains of the past generation will mean little to adults with disabilities who cannot qualify for the jobs they need to become self-supporting.

## Ethics and Genetics

Perhaps the most intriguing questions facing America in the 1990s with respect to disability have to do with the rapid advances in genetics. These breakthroughs raise troubling ethical questions, as we saw in chapter 2. Should a fetus believed to have a disability be aborted? Is there a public interest in these decisions? Should government take a position? Who has a right to genetic information?

Progress in genetics has far outpaced our understanding of the ethics of genetics. As a result, expectant parents often learn more than they know how to handle. The likelihood is for more of the same: the more information we get, the more difficult decisions seem to be. For example, we now can identify disability during the first trimester of pregnancy. The problem is that the only option the mother faces is to continue to term or abort the fetus. Medicine does not yet know how to fix the problem, replace a faulty gene, or take other steps that would help short of an abortion. The first such human genetic engineering experiments just now are beginning. It will be years, perhaps decades, before we learn enough about gene therapy to alter genes in utero and thus give expectant mothers an option other than abortion.

The major issues are: Who should make the decisions? Who should pay the costs, which are sure to be high? And where do we stop — do we only correct disabilities or do we improve upon nature? There are many factors the prospective mother probably will weigh in making this decision. Among other things, her religious convictions, her moral beliefs, her family genetics history and that of her partner — all will influence how she decides. These are good arguments for a pro-choice position: she and her partner will, after all, be responsible for the child until that child reaches majority.

If we believe that the decision should be a private and personal one involving only the prospective mother and whomever else she wants to bring in to advise her, we should take the position that society at large — and certainly government — has no role to play. But many Americans hold powerful ethical and religious beliefs that give them pause when they consider whether a prospective mother alone should make such decisions.

What about the issue of public funding for abortion of infants believed to be disabled? The federal government spends more than $100 billion each year, and government on all levels spends some three times that much annually, on programs for people with disabilities. Lifelong care for a severely disabled person who requires such assistance may cost millions of dollars — per person. Does government thus have an interest in aborting fetuses that may end up costing it huge sums of money?

Perhaps genetic engineering will help to resolve this question. In a few years, gene therapy will offer another choice: that of "fixing" the gene and thus saving the fetus. Should government fund such intervention, on the grounds that it not only enhances the quality of life for these individuals but also saves large sums of money for taxpayers? A related question is whether individuals with disabilities themselves have a right to genetic engineering, once it becomes technically feasible. Is this something for which Medicare and Medicaid should pay?

The statement is sometimes made that "No one could oppose efforts to cure disabilities." But some people do. There are, for example, many deaf people who oppose research to cure deafness. They believe that such research makes the statement that they are less good than are other people, that they should be "fixed" in

**111**

order to become as good as others. For this reason, some even talk about wanting to firebomb research labs in order to stop the research, on the grounds that the research implies that government believes that they are less than acceptable as long as they are deaf.[5] Such radical views are not shared by all hearing-impaired adults. Certainly, members of the Association of Late Deafened Adults or of the Oral Deaf Adults Section of the Bell Association would be unlikely to espouse such sentiments.

Now that geneticists can identify disability in the genes, who has the right to see the results of such tests? Does a prospective bride have the right to know that her husband-to-be has genetically caused multiple sclerosis and might become unable, perhaps two decades into the marriage, to support her? Does a prospective employer have the right to know that a would-be employee has a heart condition or is susceptible to Huntington's or Alzheimer's disease? Does a father-to-be have the right to know the genetic test information being used by the prospective mother in making an abortion decision? Do her parents have that right?

And does a person born with a disability have a right to sue his or her parents for having acted in disregard for evidence showing that he or she would be born disabled? The issue hardly is farfetched. Already, a severely disabled young person took his parents to court for having proceeded to term with him, and sought monetary damages. The court's decision, interestingly, was that the suit was moot: had the parents not made that choice, there would be no human being in court challenging them, so the son had no right to monetary damages.

There are other questions, too. Abortions performed after discovering a genetically caused disability might also end the life of someone who had much to offer the world. Some making this argument point to the high apparent correlation between genetic-based depression and other mental illnesses, on the one hand, and artistic genius on the other. Genetic engineering could have unintended effects, as well. We might, in our haste to eliminate unwanted genetic traits, deprive future generations of possible beneficial effects arising from these same genes. Our level of knowledge of genetics is not yet such that we know exactly what all our genes do. We do know that many genes act in concert with other genes. Removing one might prevent a disability, but it also might disrupt some bodily function in ways we cannot predict.

Even more troubling for many is the question of "playing God" with genes. If we can, through gene therapy, remove faulty genes and replace them with healthy genes, should we be doing that, knowing that it would surely lead, for persons with enough money to afford it, to "designer babies?"[6] People might design their children as they now decorate a house. Where would all of this end?[7]

No one can answer these questions now. Someday, however, we will face these issues and, one way or another, resolve them.[8]

# APPENDIX ONE
# LAWS ABOUT DISABILITY

The *Air Carriers Access Act* (PL 99–435), 49 U.S.C. 1301. This law, enacted in 1986, extended section 504 coverage to include airlines. Originally, section 504 applied only to airports, which received federal grants. The carriers, such as United, Delta, and Northwest, claimed that they were not required to practice nondiscrimination on the basis of disability because they were not grant recipients. The 1986 law noted that they "benefited" from the federal grants for construction and maintenance of airports, so would henceforth have to obey section 504.

The *Americans with Disabilities Act* (PL 101–336), 42 U.S.C. 12101. Enacted in 1990, ADA protects people with disabilities from discrimination in employment, in stores and theatres, and public transportation.

The *Fair Housing Amendments Act* (PL 100–430), 42 U.S.C. 3601. Enacted in 1988, it forbids discrimination on the basis of disability by realtors and landlords. All new four-unit apartment, condominium, or cooperative buildings erected after March 13, 1991, must be accessible and adaptable for people with disabilities. In addition, occupants with disabilities may make accessibility alterations in apartments at their own expense.

The *Individuals with Disabilities Education Act* (PL 101–476), 20 U.S.C. 1400. Enacted in 1975 and amended in 1990 (when the name IDEA was adopted), this law assures "a free, appropriate, public education" to every child with a disability until he or she graduates from high school or reaches the age of twenty-two.

The *Rehabilitation Act* (PL 93–112), 29 U.S.C. 794. Enacted in 1973, and amended in 1974, 1978, 1983, and 1986, the act includes section 504, which forbids discrimination on the basis of disability by any recipient of federal grants. It also includes section 503, which requires similar steps of companies holding federal contracts, and section 501, which bans discrimination in employment by federal agencies.

The *Technology Related Assistance for Individuals with Disabilities Act* (PL 100–407), 29 U.S.C. 2201. Passed in 1988, TRAIDA provides federal funds to states for expanding technology services for disabled children and adults, and for purchasing devices.

The *Television Decoder Circuitry Act* (PL 101–431), 47 U.S.C. 609; 47 U.S.C 303. Enacted in 1990, it requires that all TV sets sold or manufactured in the United States after 1993 be equipped with built-in closed-captioning chips.

# A NOTE ON THE SIZE OF THE POPULATION

**N**o one knows precisely how many Americans have disabilities. In part, this is a problem of definitions. What do we mean by "disability"? The Americans with Disabilities Act uses a three-part civil rights definition first adopted in the Rehabilitation Act Amendments of 1974: people who have permanent medical conditions preventing or limiting major life activities such as working or going to school, people who have a record of such a condition, and people falsely regarded as having such a condition. This definition works well for purposes of civil rights issues, and we as a nation have almost a generation of case law to help us to interpret it. This definition does not, however, lend itself readily to demography: it is hard to count people using this definition.

Population surveys more often use a self-report definition: people with disabilities are those who say they are. No medical examination is given in such studies. That usually is acceptable because the number of false positives (people who say they are disabled, but are not) is manageably small. This is the technique used by the Louis Harris & Associates studies quoted in this book.

Some health surveys don't refer to disabilities at all but rather to "functional limitations" or specific impairments. Thus, the National Health Interview Survey

(HIS) asks about hearing, vision, and other capacities. The problem is that impairments, generally speaking, are more mild than are disabilities. To illustrate: one may have a vision impairment, but unless it meets two tests — it is permanent (not temporary), and it is severe enough to prevent or interfere with things like working — it would not be a disability.

When Congress worked on the Americans with Disabilities Act, it relied in part on a report derived from a health status study which found that some forty-three million Americans have impairments. Overlooked at the time is the basic fact that impairments are not disabilities. Arguably, then, not all of those forty-three million people are disabled.

This book uses the estimate of thirty-six million Americans as having disabilities. That number is neither the lowest nor the highest projection quoted in professional literature, but it is somewhere in the middle range of those projections. The reader should understand that it is an estimate, as are all figures on the size of this population. The actual number could be lower or could be higher. No one knows exactly. It is quite possible that no one ever will know precisely. In the judgment of the author, it is a responsible estimate, one we can rely upon to guide us in our discussions.

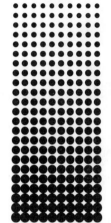

## APPENDIX THREE
# ORGANIZATIONS

**FEDERAL**

Architectural and Transportation Barriers
    Compliance Board
1331 F Street NW
Washington, DC 20004
800-USA-ABLE

A small independent federal agency offering guidelines on accessibility in construction and transportation.

Department of Education
Office of Special Education Programs
400 Maryland Avenue SW
Washington, DC 20202
202-732-1007

The federal agency responsible for administering the Individuals with Disabilities Education Act (IDEA) and other laws providing services to people with disabilities.

Department of Housing and Urban Development
451 7th Street SW
Washington, DC 20410
202-708-1422

The federal agency responsible for implementation of PL 100–407, the Fair Housing Amendments Act of 1990.

Department of Justice
Office of the Americans with Disabilities Act
Civil Rights Division
Washington, DC 20530 202-514-0301

The federal office responsible for implementation of ADA titles II (on state and local government) and III (on places of public accommodation).

Department of Transportation
Urban and Mass Transportation Administration
400 7th Street SW
Washington, DC 20590
202-366-4043

The federal office responsible for implementation of ADA transportation requirements.

Equal Employment Opportunity Commission
1801 L Street NW
Washington, DC 20507
800-669-EEOC

The federal agency responsible for implementation of ADA title I (on employment).

Federal Communications Commission
1919 M Street NW
Washington, DC 20554
202-634-7000

The federal agency responsible for implementation of ADA title IV (on telecommunications) and PL 101-431, the Television Decoder Circuitry Act of 1990 (on caption decoders in commercial TV sets).

National Council on Disability
800 Independence Avenue SW #814
Washington, DC 20591
202-267-3846

A small independent federal agency that advocates for laws for people with disabilities.

National Institutes of Health
Bethesda, MD 20892
301-402-0252

The institutes sponsor research on hearing (National Institute on Deafness and Other Communication Disorders), aging and age-related disabilities (National Institute on Aging), etc.

Social Security Administration
Department of Health and Human Services
6401 Security Boulevard
Baltimore, MD 21235
800-772-1213

The federal agency responsible for administering Social Security Disability Insurance (SSDI) and Supplemental Security Income (SSI)

### GENERAL

Disability Rights Education and Defense Fund
2032 San Pablo Avenue
Berkeley, CA 94702
415-644-2455

A private advocacy organization of and for people with disabilities.

HEATH Resource Center
American Council on Education
1 Dupont Circle #800
Washington, DC 20036
202-939-9320, or 800-544-3284

A private program offering information on higher education programs for people with disabilities.

National Easter Seals Society
70 East Lake St.
Chicago, IL 60601
312-726-6200

NESS and its two hundred affiliates nationwide are private, nonprofit providers of services for children and adults with physical disabilities.

Consortium for Citizens with Disabilities
c/o The Arc
1522 K Street NW
Washington, DC 20005
202-785-3388

An association of Washington-based advocacy groups.

### BLINDNESS/LOW VISION

American Foundation for the Blind
15 West 16th Street
New York, NY 10011
212-620-2000

Publishes a *Directory of Services for Blind and Visually Impaired Persons in the United States* which lists more than a thousand programs.

American Council of the Blind
1155 15th Street NW #720
Washington, DC 20005
202-467-5081

A consumer organization of blind and low-vision adults.

### CEREBRAL PALSY

United Cerebral Palsy Associations Inc.
1522 K Street NW #1112

Washington, DC 20005
202-842-1266

A private organization with 183 affiliates nationwide.


## DEAFNESS/HEARING IMPAIRMENT

National Association of the Deaf
814 Thayer Avenue
Silver Spring, MD 20910
301-587-1788 (voice)
301-587-1789 (TDD)

A consumer organization with state chapters nationwide.

Telecommunications for the Deaf Inc.
8719 Colesville, Suite 300
Silver Spring, MD 20910-3919
301-589-3786

A consumer and industry association interested in technology for communication-impaired persons.

Self Help for Hard of Hearing People
7800 Wisconsin Avenue
Bethesda, MD 20814
301-657-2249 (voice/TDD)

A consumer association with groups and chapters throughout the nation.


## DIABETES

American Diabetes Association
505 Eighth Avenue, 21st Floor
New York, NY 10018
212-947-9707

Offers brochures on diabetes.

Juvenile Diabetes Foundation
432 Park Avenue South
New York, NY 10016-8013
212-889-7575, or 800-JDF-CURE

Founded in 1971, it has 128 chapters in North America and funds the Diabetes Research Foundation.

### EPILEPSY

Epilepsy Foundation of America
4351 Garden City Drive
Landover, MD 20785
301-459-3700, or 800-332-1000

A private organization providing information and advocacy services for people with epilepsy.

### LEARNING DISABILITY

ACLD: An Association for Children and Adults with
    Learning Disabilities
4156 Library Road
Pittsburgh, PA 15234
412-341-1515

A parent-based group offering information and advocacy for children, youths, and adults with dyslexia and other learning disabilities.

Orton Dyslexia Society
24 York Road
Baltimore, MD 21204
301-296-0232

A private group specializing in dyslexia.

### MULTIPLE SCLEROSIS

National Multiple Sclerosis Society
733 Third Avenue
New York, NY 10017
800-624-8236 , or 800-227-3166, or 212-476-0472

A private organization sponsoring research and offering information about MS.

### MUSCULAR DYSTROPHY
Muscular Dystrophy Association
3561 East Sunrise Drive
Tucson, AZ 85718
602-529-2000

Sponsors the Labor Day Telethon, which helps support research, service, and information programs.

### RETARDATION
The Arc
500 East Border Street
Arlington, TX 76010
817-261-6003

A private, nonprofit association of affiliates providing services, information, research, and advocacy on behalf of people with retardation.

National Down Syndrome Society
666 Broadway, Suite 810
New York, NY 10012
212-460-9330, or 800-221-4602

Sponsors research, information, and outreach on behalf of children and adults with Down syndrome.

### SPEECH/LANGUAGE
American Speech Language Hearing Association
10801 Rockville Pike
Rockville, MD 20802
301-897-5700, or 800-638-8255

A professional organization for speech, language, and hearing therapists.

American Cleft Palate Association
University of Pittsburgh
331 Falk Hall
Pittsburgh, PA 15211
800-24-CLEFT

A private association offering information about speech disorders due to cleft palate.

### TRAUMATIC BRAIN INJURY
National Head Injury Foundation
1140 Connecticut Avenue NW #812
Washington, DC 20036
202-296-6443

A private organization advocating for laws benefiting people with TBI.

New Medico Head Injury System
14 Central Avenue
Lynn, MA 01901
800-CARE TBI

Publishes *Headlines*, a quarterly magazine.

### VETERANS
Disabled American Veterans
807 Maine Avenue SW
Washington, DC 20024
202-554-3501

A private organization representing more than one million disabled veterans.

Paralyzed Veterans of America
801 18th Street NW
Washington, DC 20006
202-872-1300

An advocacy group comprised of veterans with spinal cord injuries.

Eastern Paralyzed Veterans Association
75–20 Astoria Blvd.
Jackson Heights, NY 11370-1178
718-803-3782

A chapter of PVA serving the Northeast section of the country.

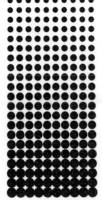

# SOURCE NOTES

**CHAPTER ONE**

1. Virginia Gallego, "Out of the Fog of Acquired Brain Injury," *Able News* (Sacramento: California Community Colleges Disabled Student Programs and Services), Spring 1989, pp. 1, 8.
2. U.S. Department of Education, *Thirteenth Annual Report on Implementation of the Individuals with Disabilities Education Act* (Washington, D.C.: Author, 1991).
3. Frank Bowe, *Adults with Disabilities: A Portrait* (Washington, D.C.: President's Committee on Employment of People with Disabilities, 1992). See also U.S. Bureau of the Census, *Labor Force Status and Other Characteristics of Persons with a Work Disability: 1981 to 1988*, Current Population Reports, Special Studies, series p-23, no. 160 (Washington, D.C.: U.S. Government Printing Office, July 1989).
4. National Head Injury Foundation, *Head Injury* (Framingham, Mass: Author, 1983). See also David Gelman, "How the Brain Recovers," *Newsweek*, April 9, 1990, pp. 48–50.
5. Frank Bowe, *Handicapping America* (New York: Harper & Row, 1978).
6. ICD/Louis Harris & Associates, *The ICD Survey of Disabled Americans. Bringing Disabled Americans into the Mainstream* (New York: International Center for the Disabled, 1986).
7. Mary MacCracken, *Turnabout Children* (Boston: Little, Brown, 1986).
8. Mitchell L. Yell, "*Honig v. Doe;* The Suspension and Expulsion of Handicapped Students," *Exceptional Children* v. 56, no. 1, pp. 60–69. See also Thomas Morgan, "Learning Disabilities and Crime: Struggling to Snap the Link," *New York Times,*

January 28, 1988, pp. Bl, B7; *Hippocrates*, March/April 1989, p. 117.

9. David Nyhan, "When Children Are Malnourished," *Boston Globe*, March 14, 1991, p. 21.

10. Uta Frith, *Autism: Explaining the Enigma* (Cambridge, Mass.: Basil Blackwell, 1989).

11. L. Rosner and S. Ross, *Multiple Sclerosis* (Englewood Cliffs, N.J.: Prentice-Hall, 1987).

12. Yvonne Baskin, "Finding the Cause of Muscular Dystrophy," *World Book Health & Medical Annual*, 1991, p. 170–83. See also "Treating Muscular Dystrophy," *World Book Science Annual*, 1991, pp. 300–301, and John Pekkanen, "Genetics: Medicine's Amazing Leap," *Reader's-Digest*, September 1991, pp. 23–32.

13. *Facts About Epilepsy* (Garden City, Md.: Epilepsy Foundation of America, undated).

14. Daniel McAlees, "Traumatic Brain Injury," *The RTC Connection* v. 8, no. 3 (November 1987).

15. Naomi Freundlich, "How Do You Mend a Broken Brain?" *Business Week*, July 8, 1991, pp. 70–71.

16. Peter Marks, "The Long Road Back," *Newsday*, September 7, 1989, pp. 4–5, 12.

17. See, for example, Jane Gross, "A Life Defiant Despite AIDS," *New York Times*, January 25, 1988, pp. Bl, B4, and Bruce Ingersoll, "FDA Asked to Clear Drug for Blindness Related to AIDS," *Wall Street Journal*, May 3, 1989, p. B3.

### CHAPTER TWO

1. *From ADA to Empowerment: The Report of the Task Force on the Rights and Empowerment of Americans with Disabilities* (Washington, D.C.: Task Force, 1991).

2. NOD/Louis Harris & Associates, *Public Attitudes Toward People with Disabilities* (Washington, D.C.: National Organization on Disability, 1991).

3. For a summary of the study, see Frank Bowe, *Rehabilitating America* (New York: Harper & Row, 1980), pp. 12–16.

4. Copies of the Rehabilitation Act Amendments of 1974 and of the Americans with Disabilities Act of 1990 are available by writing to your congressman (U.S. House of Representatives, Washington, D.C. 20515) or to your senator (U.S. Senate, Washington, D.C. 20510).

5. Frank Bowe, *Adults with Disabilities: A Portrait* (Washington, D.C.: President's Committee on Employment of People with Disabilities, 1992). See also U.S. Bureau of the Census, *Labor*

*Force Status and Other Characteristics of Persons with a Work Disability: 1981 to 1988.* Current Population Reports, Special Studies, series P-23, no. 160 (Washington, D.C.: U.S. Government Printing Office, July 1989).

6. Harris, *Public Attitudes*, vii, ix.
7. D. Besharov, "Does Drug Abuse Equal Child Abuse?" Newsday, April 15, 1991, p. 39. See also Suzanne Daley, "Born on Crack and Coping with Kindergarten," *New York Times*, February 7, 1991, pp. Al, D24; Jane Schneider, Dan Griffith, and Ira Chasnoff, "Infants Exposed to Cocaine in Utero: Implications for Developmental Assessment and Intervention," *Infants and Young Children*, July 1989, pp. 25–36; and National Council on Disability, "HHS Releases Report on Crack Babies," *Focus*, Spring 1990, pp. 1, 8.
8. Barbara Kantrowitz, "The Crack Children," *Newsweek*, February 12, 1990, pp. 62–63.
9. B. D. Colen, "Cocaine Babies," *Newsday*, March 27, 1990, pp. 1, 7.
10. Michael Hinds, "Use of Crack Is Said to Stifle the Instincts of Parenthood," *New York Times*, March 17, 1990, p. 8.
11. "HHS Releases Report on Crack Babies," *Focus*, Spring 1990, pp. 1, 8.
12. Jamie Talan, "Study on Coke Babies Cites Environment," *Newsday*, May 16, 1991, p. 38.
13. Gina Kolata, "A New Toll of Alcohol Abuse: The Indians' Next Generation," *New York Times*, July 19, 1989, pp. Al, D24.
14. Elizabeth Rosenthal, "When a Pregnant Woman Drinks," *New York Times Magazine*, February 4, 1990, pp. 30, 49, 61.
15. "When Dad Drinks," *Scientific American*, February 1990, p. 23.
16. Michael Waldholz, "Newer Prenatal Test, Performed Earlier on Fetus, Poses Only Slightly More Risk," *Wall Street Journal*, March 9, 1989, p. B5.
17. D. Haney, "Gene Linked to Retardation Discovered," *Washington Post*, May 30, 1991, p. A6.
18. Jerry Bishop, "Genes Are Found That May Predispose Some Families to Get Multiple Sclerosis," *Wall Street Journal*, June 30, 1989, p. B2.
19. Stephen Hall, "The Gene-Boy," *Hippocrates*, November–December 1989, pp. 75–82.
20. Robert Cooke, "2 Diabetes Genes Tracked in Mice," *Newsday*, June 13, 1991, 41.
21. _____, "Experts Debating Gene Therapy," *Newsday*, May 21, 1991, pp. 59, 61.

22. Geoffrey Montgomery, "The Ultimate Medicine," Discover, March 1990, pp. 60–62, 64, 66–68.
23. Geoffrey Cowley, "Made to Order Babies," *Newsweek*, Special Edition, Winter/Spring 1990, pp. 94–95, 98, 100.

### CHAPTER THREE

1. *From ADA to Empowerment: The Report of the Task Force on the Rights and Empowerment of Americans with Disabilities* (Washington, D.C.: Task Force, 1991).
2. Nancy Mairs, *Carnal Acts: Essays* (New York: HarperCollins, 1990).
3. ICD/Louis Harris & Associates, *The ICD Survey of Disabled Americans: Bringing Disabled Americans into the Mainstream* (New York: International Center for the Disabled, 1986).
4. U.S. Architectural and Transportation Barriers Compliance Board, "ATBCB Recommends More Access to Capitol Buildings," *Access America*, Fall/Winter 1990, p. 6.
5. U.S. Department of Education, *Thirteenth Annual Report on Implementation of the Individuals with Disabilities Education Act* (Washington, D.C.: Author, 1991).
6. *Information from HEATH* (Washington, DC: American Council on Education, Fall 1990), p. 3.
7. NOD/Louis Harris & Associates, *Public Attitudes Toward People with Disabilities* (Washington, D.C.: National Organization on Disability, 1991) pp. 9–12.
8. Frank Bowe, *Handicapping America* (New York: Harper & Row, 1978).
9. ICD/Louis Harris & Associates, *ICD III: A Report Card on Special Education* (New York: International Center for the Disabled, 1989).
10. *Sullivan v. Zebley et al.* Supreme Court, February 20, 1990, No. 88–1377. See also, Spencer Rich, "Thousands of Children in Line for Aid," *Washington Post*, March 1, 1990, p. A23.
11. John Pekkanen, "Genetics: Medicine's Amazing Leap," *Reader's Digest*, September 1991, pp. 23–32. See also, Yvonne Baskin, "Finding the Cause of Muscular Dystrophy," *World Book Health & Medical Annual*, 1991, and "Treating Muscular Dystrophy," *World Book Science Annual*, 1991, pp. 300–301.
12. Stephen Hall, "The Gene Boy," *Hippocrates*, November/December 1989, pp. 75–82.
13. "Raping Justice," *Tampa Tribune*, May 12, 1989, pp. 18-A.
14. Michael Slackman, "'It's a Fight for Rights,'" *Newsday*, September 4, 1991, pp. 3, 25.
15. Virginia Gallego, "Out of the Fog of Acquired Brain Injury,"

*Able News* (Sacramento: California Community Colleges Disabled Student Programs and Services), Spring 1989, pp. 1, 8.

16. Timothy O'Brien, "Disabled Get New Weapons in Battle Against Discrimination," *Newsday*, September 1, 1991, pp. 106–7.

17. "The Man Who Used 29 Names," *Newsday*, September 2, 1991, p. 8.

18. Paul Vitello, "Looking Out for Big Brother," *Newsday*, March 26, 1991, p. 6.

19. Irene Virag, "Harnessing the Struggle in Her Life," *Newsday*, May 16, 1990, p. 21.

### CHAPTER FOUR

1. *Timothy W. v. Rochester. New Hampshire School District*, 875 F:2nd 954 (lst Cir. 1989), 15 EHLR 441:393.

2. Carolee Reiling, *How Significant Is "Significant"?* (Columbus, Ohio: Association on Handicapped Student Service Programs in Postsecondary Education, 1990).

3. Alison Sutton, "I Wish I Knew Then, What I Know Now," *Shhh*, July/August 1990.

4. P.L. 101-476 is the Education of the Handicapped Act Amendments of 1990, amending the 1970 Education of the Handicapped Act and the 1975 Education for All Handicapped Children Act, PL 941-142.

5. P.L. 93-112, 29 U.S.C. 794, September 26, 1973.

6. U.S. Department of Education, *Thirteenth Annual Report on Implementation of the Individuals with Disabilities Education Act* (Washington; D.C.: Author, 1991), pp. xv.

7. Ibid, p. xxi.

8. Michael D'Antonio, "Battle Looms Over Special Ed," *Newsday*, January 16, 1989, pp. 7, 21.

9. U.S. Department of Education, *Thirteenth Annual*, xvi.

10. *Information from HEATH* (Washington, D.C. American Council on Education, June/July 1991) p. 7. See also Stimola, below.

11. Michael Stimola, "Accessibility and the New York State College and University System," *Momentum*, Winter 1991, pp. 22–30.

12. Frank Bowe, *Handicapping America* (New York: Harper & Row, 1978).

13. 348 F. Supp. 866 (D.D.C. 1972).

14. 343 F. Supp. 279 (E.D.Pa. 1972).

15. U.S. Department of Education, *Twelfth Annual Report on Implementation of the Education of the Handicapped Act* (Washington, D.C.: Author; 1990), pp. 78–85.

16. Ibid.
17. Frank Bowe, *Adults with Disabilities: A Portrait* (Washington, D.C.: President's Committee on Employment of People with Disabilities, 1992. See also U.S. Bureau of the Census, *Labor Force Status and Other Characteristics of Persons with a Work Disability: 1981 to 1988*, Current Population Reports, Special Studies, series P-23, no. 160 (Washington, D.C.: U.S. Government Printing Office, July 1989).
18. U.S. Department of Education, *Thirteenth Annual Report on Implementation of the Individuals with Disabilities Education Act* (Washington, D.C.: Author, 1991).
19. Ibid.
20. ICD/Louis Harris & Associates, *ICD III: A Report Card on Special Education* (New York: International Center for the Disabled, 1989).
21. Frank Bowe, *Approaching Equality* (Silver Spring, Md.: TJ Publishers, 1991).

### CHAPTER FIVE

1. Wayne J. Smith, "Bye, Bye Bus Industry," *New York Times*, November 30, 1989.
2. "Busing In Higher Costs," editorial, *Wall Street Journal*, November 20, 1989.
3. James Weisman, "Cooperating and Marketing Are Key to Successful Accessible Transit," *Project Action Update* Winter 1991, p. 5. See also "Wheelchair Accessible New York City Subway Stations with Detailed Information About Neighborhood Connecting Accessible Bus Routes and Commuter Rail Stations," a pamphlet published by Weisman's EPVA.
4. Weisman, p. 3.
5. American Public Transit Association, *Transit: Meeting the Mobility Needs of Elderly and Disabled People* (Washington, D.C.: Author, 1985).
6. C. Kerr and L. Lally, *National Urban Mass Transportation Statistics, 1985 Section 15 Annual Report* (Washington, D.C.: Urban Mass Transportation Administration, 1987).
7. David Pfeiffer, "Public Transit Access for Disabled Persons in the United States," *Disability, Handicap & Society* v. 5, no. 2 (1990): pp. 153–66.
8. NOD/Louis Harris & Associates, *Public Attitudes Toward People with Disabilities* (Washington, D.C.: National Organization on Disability, 1991), pp. 64–65.
9. Frank Bowe, "Accessible Transportation," in N. Crews, I. Zola,

and Associates, eds., *Independent Living for Physically Disabled People* (San Francisco: Jossey-Bass, 1983).

10. "Transportation for Individuals with Disabilities," *Federal Register*, October 4, 1990, pp. 40762–40782.
11. Because the Air Carriers Access Act (PL 99–435), 49 U.S.C. 1301, adequately completed the federal task of assuring access to air transportation, the Americans with Disabilities Act did not address air travel.
12. Frank Bowe, *Rehabilitating America* (New York: Harper & Row, 1980).
13. Dennis Cannon, "Transit Providers Want Definition of 'Common Wheelchair,'" *Project Action Update*, Winter 1991, pp. 5–6.
14. Susan Perry, "Absorbing Costs of ADA Problematic for Intercity Bus Systems," *Project Action Update*, Spring 1991, pp. 5.
15. Weisman, pp. 3–4.
16. Robert Ashby, "Transit Providers Will Limit Traditionally Broad-based Paratransit Eligibility," *Project Action Update*, Winter 1991, p. 10.
17. Jack Gilstrap, "Transit Systems and Consumers Share Goal: Best Possible Service for Lowest Possible Fare," *Project Action Update*, Spring 1991, p. 3.

### CHAPTER SIX

1. Ruth Marcus, "U.S. Alleges Housing Bias Against Handicapped," *Washington Post*, June 21, 1989, p. A9.
2. Elizabeth Wasserman, "After Arson, Home Finds Acceptance," *Newsday*, September 24, 1989, pp. NHW 1, 3.
3. John Kemp, personal communication, August 30, 1991.
4. Frank Bowe, "Into the Private Sector: Rights and People with Disabilities," Journal of Disability Policy Studies v. 1, no. 1, (1990): 87–99.
5. Fair Housing Amendments Act (PL 100–430), 42 U.S.C. 3601.
6. Jane Lehman, "Housing Debate: How Will Handicapped Fit In?" *Newsday*, May 19, 1990, p. 7.
7. Patricia Moore, personal communication, November 1, 1991.
8. Susan Howard, "Resistance to Proposed Group Home," *Newsday*, February 27, 1990, p. 27.
9. Peter Marks, "They Say No," *Newsday*, May 20, 1990, pp. 5, 26.
10. "Build Those Group Homes Despite Local Protest," *Newsday*, September 2, 1988, p. 80.
11 Marks "They Say No."
12. NOD/Louis Harris & Associates, *Public Attitudes Toward People*

with *Disabilities* (Washington, D.C.: National Organization on Disability, 1991), pp. 18, 31.

13. Jerry Adler and Lisa Drew, "Waking Sleeping Souls," *Newsweek,* March 28, 1988, pp. 70–71.
14. Charles Lakin, "History, Philosophy, and Prevailing Practices of Long-term Care for Mentally Retarded People," unpublished manuscript, University of Minnesota, 1988. See also Peter Marks, "Inside LI's 1st Group Home," *Newsday,* May 21, 1990, pp. 7, 22–23.
15. Michael Hinds, "Suit Over Care for Retarded May Bring Wider Challenges," *New York Times,* September 5, 1989, pp. Al, A12. See also Adler and Drew, "Waking Sleeping Souls."
16. Ann Braden Johnson, *Out of Bedlam: The Truth about Deinstitutionalization* (New York: Basic Books, 1990).
17. Jim Puzzanghera, "Aid for Disabled at Home," *Newsday,* August 31, 1991, p. 4.
18. Hinds, "Suit Over Care for Retarded."
19. Ibid.
20. Beverly Lawrence, "Breaking the Barriers," *Newsday,* February 28, 1991, pp. 71, 75.
21. Ibid.
22. *Assessment of Housing Needs for Persons with Disabilities and Traumatic Brain Injury in Nassau and Suffolk Counties* (Hempstead, N.Y.: Coma Recovery Association, 1989).
23. Christopher Kenneally, "For the Disabled, Housing Remains a Challenge," *Boston Globe,* November 3, 1990, p. 45.

### CHAPTER SEVEN

1. *ICD/Louis Harris & Associates Survey of Disabled Americans: Bringing Disabled Americans into the Mainstream* (New York: International Center for the Disabled, 1986).
2. Stephen Holmes, "Disabled People Say Home Care Is Needed to Use New Rights," *New York Times,* October 14, 1990.
3. Frank Bowe, *Adults with Disabilities: A Portrait* (Washington, D.C.: President's Committee on Employment of People with Disabilities, 1991. See also U.S. Bureau of the Census, *Labor Force Status and Other Characteristics of Persons with a Work Disability: 1981 to 1988,* Current Population Reports, Special Studies, series p-23, no. 160 (Washington, D.C.: U.S. Government Printing Office, July 1989).
4. *Workforce 2000* (Indianapolis: Hudson Institute, 1987).
5. Frank Bowe, "Into the Private Sector: Rights and People with

Disabilities," *Journal of Disability Policy Studies* v. 1, no. 1 (1990): 87–99.

6. U.S. Equal Employment Opportunity Commission, "Equal Employment Opportunity for Individuals with Disabilities; Final Rule," *Federal Register*, July 26, 1991, p. 35739.

7. John Kemp, personal communication, August 30, 1991. Mr. Kemp (no relation to Evan Kemp) assisted the EEOC chairman in preparing the testimony.

8. Steven Holmes, "Disabled People Say Home Care Is Needed to Use New Rights," *New York Times*, October 14, 1990.

### CHAPTER EIGHT

1. *From ADA to Empowerment; The Report of the Task Force on the Rights and Empowerment of Americans with Disabiltities* (Washington, D.C.: Task Force, 1991).

2. U.S. Department of Justice, "Nondiscrimination on the Basis of Disability by Public Accommodations and in Commercial Facilities; Final Rule," *Federal Register*, July 26, 1991, p. 35601.

3. Ibid., 35597.

4. *ICD/Louis Harris & Associates Survey of Disabled Americans: Bringing Disabled Americans into the Mainstream* (New York: International Center for the Disabled, 1986).

5. American Broadcasting Company, "Response to Notice of Draft Recommendations 1," U.S. Congress Commission on Education of the Deaf, #242, December 11, 1987. Summarized in Frank Bowe, *Approaching Equality* (Silver Spring, Md.: TJ Publishers, 1991).

6. National Captioning Institute, "Statement to U.S. Congress Commission on Education of the Deaf," March 17, 1987. Summarized in Bowe, *Approaching Equality*.

7. PL 101–431, the Television Decoder Circuitry Act of 1990, 47 U.S.C. 303, October 16, 1990.

8. R. Ferguson, "Law May Soon Ease Access to Captioned TV for Deaf," *Wall Street Journal*, August 22, 1990, pp. B1, B4.

9. PL 101–376, the Individuals with Disabilities Education Act, 20 U.S.C. 1400, October 30, 1990.

10. Social Security Administration, *SSI: Supplemental Security Income* (Baltimore: Author, 1991). See also *A Summary Guide to Social Security and Supplemental Security Income Work Incentives for the Disabled and Blind* (Baltimore: Social Security Administration, 1988).

11. Spencer Rich, "Thousands of Children in Line for Aid," *Washington Post*, March 1, 1990, p. A23.

12. Frank Bowe, *Adults with Disabilities: A Portrait* (Washington, D.C.: President's Committee on Employment of People with Disabilities, 1992). See also U.S. Bureau of the Census, *Labor Force Status and Other Characteristics of Persons with a Work Disability: 1981 to 1988*, Current Population Reports, Special Studies, series p-23, no. 160 (Washington, D.C.: U.S. Government Printing Office, July 1989).

**CHAPTER NINE**

1. *From ADA to Empowerment: The Report of the Task Force on the Rights and Empowerment of Americans with Disabilities* (Washington, D.C.: Task Force, 1991).
2. Frank Bowe, *Handicapping America* (New York: Harper & Row, 1978).
3. Frank Bowe, *Comeback* (New York: Harper & Row, 1981).

**CHAPTER TEN**

1. Ellen Yan, "His Secret Is Looking Forward," *Newsday*, September 3, 1991, p. 25.
2. Frank Bowe, *Rehabilitating America* (New York: Harper & Row, 1980).
3. John Kemp, personal communication, August 30, 1991.
4. Robert Davila, personal communication, August 12, 1991.
5. Frank Bowe, *Approachinq Equality* (Silver Spring, Md.: TJ Publishers. 1991).
6. Geoffrey Cowley, "Made to Order Babies," *Newsweek*, Special Edition, Winter/Spring 1990, pp. 94–95, 98, 100.
7. Gina Kolata, "Why Gene Therapy Is Considered Scary, but Cell Therapy Isn't," *New York Times*, September 16, 1990, p. E5.
8. Alan Otten, "Parental Agony," *Wall Street Journal*, March 8, 1989, pp. A1, A8.

# FOR FURTHER READING

Ballard, Joseph, et al. *P.L. 94–142. Section 504, and P.L. 99–457: Understanding What They Are.* Reston, Va.: Council for Exceptional Children, 1987.

Berkowitz, Edward, ed. *Disability Policies and Government Programs.* New York: Praeger, 1979.

Berkowitz, Edward. *Disabled Policy: America's Programs for the Handicapped.* New York: Cambridge University Press, 1987.

Bowe, Frank. *Handicapping America: Barriers to Disabled People.* New York: Harper & Row, 1978.

Bullock, Lyndal, ed. *Exceptionalities in Children and Youth.* Boston: Allyn and Bacon, 1992.

Bureau of National Affairs. *The Americans with Disabilities Act: A Practice and Legal Guide to Impact, Enforcement and Compliance.* Washington, D.C.: Author, 1990.

ICD/Louis Harris & Associates. *ICD III: A Report Card on Special Education.* New York: International Center for the Disabled, 1989.

ICD/Louis Harris & Associates. *The ICD Survey of Disabled Americans: Bringing Disabled Americans into the Mainstream.* New York: International Center for the Disabled, 1986.

Mueller, James. *The Workplace Workbook: An Illustrated Guide to Job Accommodation and Assistive Technology.* Washington, D.C.: The Dole Foundation, 1990.

NOD/Louis Harris & Associates. *Public Attitudes Toward People with Disabilities.* Washington, D.C.: National Organization on Disability, 1991.

U.S. Department of Education. *Thirteenth Annual Report on Implementation of the Individuals with Disabilities Education Act.* Washington, D.C.: Author, 1991.

West, Jane, ed. *The Americans with Disabilities Act: From Policy to Practice.* New York: Millbank Memorial Fund, 1991.

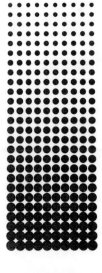

# INDEX

**143**

# ABOUT THE AUTHOR

**F**rank Bowe, a professor of counseling research in the Special Education and Rehabilitation Department at Hofstra University, has long been active in the pursuit of equal rights for Americans with disabilities. He has been regional commissioner of the Rehabilitation Services Administration for the U.S. Department of Education, chairperson of the U.S. Congress Commission on Education of the Deaf, executive director of the American Coalition of Citizens with Disabilities, and a special representative to the United Nations. Dr. Bowe has advanced degrees from Gallaudet University and New York University and is the author of numerous articles, reports, and books, including *Handicapping America, Personal Computers and Special Needs, Approaching Equality,* and *Changing the Rules.* He received the Distinguished Service Award of the President of the United States in 1992 in recognition of more than fifteen years of contributions to American public policy on disability. Dr. Bowe lives on Long Island, New York, with his wife, Phyllis, and daughters, Doran and Whitney.